ON THE
CROSS
ROAD

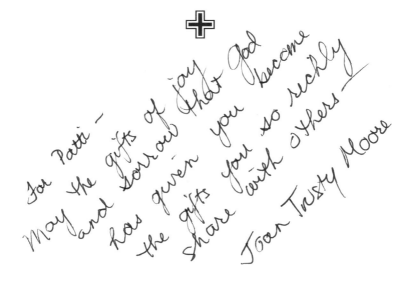

For Patti —
May the gifts of joy
and sorrow that God
has given you become
the gifts you so richly
share with others —

Joan Trusty Moore

ON THE
CROSS
ROAD

A Daily Devotional for Lent

Joan Trusty Moore

Judson Press
Valley Forge

On the Cross Road: A Daily Devotional for Lent
© 1999 by Judson Press, Valley Forge, PA 19482-0851
All rights reserved.

Bible quotations in this volume are from the Revised Standard
Version of the Bible copyright © 1946, 1952, 1971, by the Di-
vision of Christian Education of the National Council of the
Churches of Christ in the U.S.A. Used by permission.

Library of Congress Cataloging-in-Publication Data

Moore, Joan Trusty.
    On the cross road : a daily devotional for Lent / Joan Trusty
Moore.
      p.   cm.
   ISBN 0-8170-1316-4 (pbk. : alk. paper)
   1. Lent – Prayer-books and devotions – English. 2. Holy week –
Prayer-books and devotions – English. 3. Easter – Prayer-books and
devotions – English. 4. Bible N.T. Gospels – Devotional literature.
I. Title.
BV85.M58 1999
242′.34 – dc21   98-50657

Printed in the U.S.A.
06	05	04	03	02	01	00	99
5	4	3	2	1			

Thank you, Scott and Paige,
for all that you are
and all the light and love you give.
Being a part of your lives
is a great gift from God indeed.

Contents

Acknowledgments

No creative work is brought to life on its own. There are always nurturers and midwives who help bring something new into the world. And so it is with those who have helped through the years, with great encouragement and reenforcement. A work of faith also is born out of learning the lessons of faith, and there are those as well who have been there through some of the hardest, darkest, most painful times in my life when faith and holding on to faith were difficult challenges indeed. My deepest thanks and gratitude go to my dad, Francis Trusty, who taught me to think and to question, and to my mom, Phyllis Trusty, who taught me to see and whose writing is among the best I have ever read. Great love and appreciation as well go to others in my family, who have all helped in ways they may not even know: Bob and Nancy Trusty, Ryan Trusty, Drew Trusty, David and Janet Trusty, Meredith Trusty, Meghan Trusty, Ed and Norma Moore, Randy Moore, Muriel U'Ren Sweeney, Sam and Nancy Sweeney, Barbara Sweeney Fanger, Lyle and Anne Trusty, and Craig and Holly Groner. Thanks also to my wonderful "extended family" of encouragers: Nancy Sharp Voith, Charlene Underhill, Jon and Doreen Lew, Marcy and Steve Hannah, Suzanne Baker, Penny Pasquesi Kuhnmuench, Renee Maciejewski, Jane Capek, Jill DeJonge, Deanna Sarvis, Rick Babb, Nancy Nelms, Paul and Laura Whitmore, Paul and Fran Walker, Lindy Sayward, Bill and Marcia Soellner, Art and Jackie Stevens, Cindy Pearson Turner, Nancy Quinn, Tracy Savage, Kathy Kurkjian, Lisa Dos Passos Benzing, Paula Angelo, and my fellow writers at the *Victoria* magazine writer's retreat with Madeleine L'Engle in October 1995. Great gratitude also goes to Margaret Chappell, who insisted on my best; to Ellen Merrick Petrill, who taught me to use the skills God gives us; to Louisa Cardenas, who taught me to edit; to Dr. Myron J. Taylor, who taught me the Bible; and to Chuie Yuen and Mary Jane Chase, who provided me refuge when it was most needed. However, this book would not have been created had it not been for the specific request of Diane Fleming, the support of my current pastor, Dr. Stephen Jones, Rev. James Davison, and Edith Davison, Rev. Deborah Hughes, Nancy Naybors and the Deacon Ministries Team, and the wonderful friends and members of First Baptist Church of Birmingham, Michigan. My husband and friend, Scott Moore, provided spiritual support, a critical sounding board, a great library, and the loving freedom to create in my own very messy fashion. And my deeply loved, not-yet-reading daughter, Paige, kept me going with "This is a great book, Mom! Is it done yet? Where are the pictures?" Heartfelt thanks to you all.

JOAN TRUSTY MOORE

Introduction

Our lives are divided into before the cross and after the cross. Whatever came before the cross was different from whatever comes after the cross. To be on the Cross Road is to be approaching that point when your life divides: this is who I was before the cross, and this is who I am now that I know the cross.

The stories of people who encountered Jesus during the last few weeks of his life make the Passion story real, personal, intimate. The panorama of the last weeks is filled with stories of individual lives changed and of choices made, as well as with stories of crowds and how their collective presence made history. Life went on in its very dailiness, even as the intrigues and great designs swirled about, even as the crescendo built. The persons who met Jesus brought to him the present reality of their lives, their hearts, their souls, all that they were and all that they could be . . . and somehow nothing was ever the same again. We see a Jesus who cared about and loved and challenged both those of the highest status and those of the lowest echelons of society, both those whose names we know and those whose names have gone unrecorded. But just as we see the stories of those individuals on the Cross Road, so also we see Jesus living out the last weeks of his time on earth, feeling keenly all that it means to be human and yet trusting with intimate confidence in his God that all would fulfill God's divine purpose and calling.

With hopes that we will find in the stories of those on the Cross Road a portion of God's truth and healing power for our own lives, this book is intended to be read as a daily devotional guide during the Lenten season. Time might be set aside for reading the listed Scripture first and then the thoughts on the passage. Although the forty days of Lent do not usually include Sundays, I have nonetheless included a devotion for every day from Ash Wednesday to Easter Saturday. I hope that as you read you will also find yourself on the Cross Road, meeting Jesus along the way.

On the Road
to Jerusalem

Mark 10:32–34

*And they were on the road, going up to Jerusa-
lem, and Jesus was walking ahead of them; and
they were amazed, and those who followed were
afraid. And taking the twelve again, he began
to tell them what was to happen to him, saying, "Behold, we are going up to Jerusalem; and
the Son of man will be delivered to the chief
priests and the scribes, and they will condemn
him to death, and deliver him to the Gentiles;
and they will mock him, and spit upon him, and
scourge him, and kill him; and after three days
he will rise."*

Jerusalem.

The holy city, the center of Jewish faith, the home
of the temple of the Lord. A place to which pilgrim-
ages were made by faithful Jews. A place infused with

the history and spiritual life of the Jewish people. To go up to Jerusalem would be to go where the spiritual was made real, where living encyclopedias of the Law walked on the streets beside you, where all of your faith centered, where atonement was possible and the Law could be fulfilled. Was this the Jerusalem to which Jesus went?

"Behold, we are going up to Jerusalem; and the Son of man will be delivered to the chief priests and the scribes, and they will condemn him to death, and deliver him to the Gentiles; and they will mock him, and spit upon him, and scourge him, and kill him; and after three days he will rise."

This was the Jerusalem at the end of the road that Jesus walked. Jerusalem was where he would be betrayed, turned in to the authorities of his own religion, and then handed over to the Roman government. In Jerusalem, he would be humiliated, tortured, and put to death. And knowing all that, Jesus continued to walk the road to Jerusalem because he knew that in Jerusalem he would fulfill God's purpose for his life — and find resurrection. Jesus had courage, yes. Jesus had a certainty that this was God's will. And Jesus had unshakable faith that out of his death would come salvation for all who believe.

L LOYD J. OGILVIE WRITES, "We, too, have a Jerusalem. It's that person, problem, or perplexity that we would rather not face. It's the realm of resistance, hostility, conflict. We can understand what Jesus went through in those last days on the way up to and into Jerusalem only if we focus on *our* Jerusalem. . . . To go into Jerusalem with Jesus is to see our lives and our society through his eyes. Where are the contradictions, the distortions, the injustices?"[1]

Have we ever been on the road to Jerusalem? And what is our Jerusalem?

Perhaps our Jerusalem is every place we've found where the golden ideal has been replaced by an illusion of fool's gold. Where hope has failed, and opportunism and cynicism have thrived. Where corruption has blossomed, and we have accepted it. Have you ever seen with the eyes of Jesus, "hurt with the heart of Jesus"? If so, you have found Jerusalem. Jesus saw the reality of Jerusalem, and yet he saw beyond the reality, saw that even those who would betray, torture, and kill him were people for whom he was called to die. Do we go ahead into our Jerusalem, knowing that we will find the unlovable, the impossible, and the unpleasant? And do we trust that in Jerusalem God will also bring redemption and resurrection?

> *Help us, Lord,*
> *to have courage and faith*
> *to enter our Jerusalem and find you there.*

Jesus on the Way to Jerusalem

Mark 10:32–34

And they were on the road, going up to Jerusalem, and Jesus was walking ahead of them; and they were amazed, and those who followed were afraid. And taking the twelve again, he began to tell them what was to happen to him, saying, "Behold, we are going up to Jerusalem; and the Son of man will be delivered to the chief priests and the scribes, and they will condemn him to death, and deliver him to the Gentiles; and they will mock him, and spit upon him, and scourge him, and kill him; and after three days he will rise."

Each of us steps onto the Cross Road because of Jesus, and we find the way filled with others so called. We cannot learn from our fellow travelers, though, watching them like a psychiatrist peering through a one-way mirror. We must also bring ourselves into an encounter with them and with Jesus, the one whom we are following down the Cross Road. As Jesus begins his journey toward Jerusalem, he continually provides glimpses of what is to come to his disciples, inviting them to see into the future along with him, to anticipate and understand not only what is going to happen, but what those events mean, and how they will be called upon to react. Yet as we see in the period between Good Friday and Easter Sunday, the disciples in fact were not ready for what happened; they were profoundly incapable of responding to and understanding the events, despite all of Jesus' efforts to help them prepare.

Since it is clear that Jesus knew what lay ahead of him in Jerusalem, why did he in fact continue down that road, why did he not turn around and continue his mission and ministry? Or, alternatively, why did he not enter Jerusalem quietly, attend the Passover like a faithful Jew, and then leave?

We often read in the Bible the phrase "in the fullness of time." The time had come. The message of Jesus needed to be taken to a higher level, one that revealed what God was telling humankind in Jesus — a message that could no longer be contained by Jesus going from town to town, followed by a retinue of seekers and believers. The message had to be shouted from the larger stage, written in bold capital letters. Jesus moved toward Jerusalem with the resoluteness of one who has finished his preparations, for whom the time has arrived to implement all that has been planned and prepared.

HAVE WE LEARNED HOW TO MOVE from the safety of planning and preparation into action? Are we in close enough contact with our God to know when all the experience and wisdom we have acquired in life have prepared us for the work to which we have been called? Are we willing to trust that the Lord will provide — even as we feel our own inadequacies very keenly? God equips us to do the work to which he calls us. And in many ways, we do know when our time comes. Sometimes, though, we hesitate, then shake our heads, turn our backs, and refuse to do what we are called to do for fear of the personal cost to ourselves. We fail to use what we have been enriched with by God. And so we refuse to get on the road to our Jerusalem, a road that may demand the highest and best of all that we have.[2] Are we willing to follow God as far as Bethany, where we find refuge with those who love us, but find ourselves unwilling to step out from that comfort into the wider, more demanding place?

> *God, help us to dare, like Jesus,*
> *to set foot on the Cross Road.*

Zacchaeus

Luke 19:1–10

He entered Jericho and was passing through. And there was a man named Zacchaeus; he was a chief tax collector, and rich. And he sought to see who Jesus was, but could not, on account of the crowd, because he was small of stature. So he ran on ahead and climbed up into a sycamore tree to see him, for he was to pass that way. And when Jesus came to the place, he looked up and said to him, "Zacchaeus, make haste and come down; for I must stay at your house to-day." So he made haste and came down, and received him joyfully. And when they saw it they all murmured, "He has gone in to be the guest of a man who is a sinner." And Zacchaeus stood and said to the Lord, "Behold, Lord, the half of my goods I give to the poor; and if I have defrauded any one of anything, I restore it four-fold." And Jesus said to him, "Today salvation has come to this house, since he is also a son of

*Abraham. For the Son of man came to seek and
to save the lost."*

The taxes to be paid to the Romans in New Testament times were onerous and many. There were taxes on everyone over a certain age for the privilege of being alive, a "ground tax," which ranged from 10 percent to 20 percent of crops, an income tax of 1 percent, a tax for use of the roads or the market, a tax on each wheel of a cart and the oxen that pulled it, a sales tax, and other discretionary taxes that a tax collector could charge at any time. Despised as a traitor, a tax collector was barred from the synagogue and was classed together with robbers and murderers. Jericho was a very wealthy and important town, one of the greatest tax collection centers in Palestine, and the chief tax collector for Jericho would have had many opportunities to "make a living."

A small man, Zacchaeus courageously entered the crowd to try to see Jesus, even though the crowd would probably take every opportunity to "accidentally" kick, trip, or elbow him and certainly would not have made it easy for him to see. So Zacchaeus shed his dignity and climbed a nearby tree to see Jesus as he passed along the road. When Jesus called him by name and said he was inviting himself to Zacchaeus's house, the most hated man in Jericho flushed with pride and immediately ran to make the needed preparations. The crowd murmured, perplexed at why Jesus would enter the house of a man who was barred from entering a house of worship. Yet Zacchaeus was so changed that he immediately promised to give half of his goods to the poor and to make a fourfold restitution, far beyond what the law demanded, if he had defrauded anyone. Jesus, at the end of his visit with Zacchaeus, said that the Son of Man had come to seek and to save the lost.

In the New Testament, the word "lost" often has the common definition, something that is not where it ought to be.[3] Zacchaeus was a lost man in that sense. He had wealth but no place, no faith community, no friends. Zacchaeus was so hungry for a place, that he, one of the wealthiest men in Jericho, clambered up a tree to see a rabbi. Zacchaeus was desperate to find his right place.

Do WE HAVE A "RIGHT PLACE" TO BE? We see throughout Jesus' ministry more than a few discussions about the rightful place for people: two of the disciples believed their rightful places were on the right and the left hand of Jesus in his kingdom, others saw children as having no place at the foot of Jesus, Mary of Bethany found a place listening to Jesus, others left homes and family to be with Jesus. Do we not all want a home, a place where we are known and loved and accepted? So many seek a place that does just that. When we are lost, we are not in the place we should be. Our place is at the foot of the Master, our place is on the Cross Road, our place is at the base of the cross, our place is wherever there is one who needs Christ. And when we have found the place where God has called us to be, then we will be home.

> *God, help us to seek you out at all cost,*
> *to find our place with you,*
> *not to rest until we have found*
> *where you would have us to be.*

Two Blind Men on the Road

Matthew 20:29–34

*And as they went out of Jericho, a great crowd
followed him. And behold, two blind men sitting by the roadside, when they heard that Jesus
was passing by, cried out, "Have mercy on us,
Son of David!" The crowd rebuked them, telling
them to be silent; but they cried out the more,
"Lord, have mercy on us, Son of David!" And
Jesus stopped and called them, saying, "What
do you want me to do for you?" They said to
him, "Lord, let our eyes be opened." And Jesus
in pity touched their eyes, and immediately they
received their sight and followed him.*

Sitting on the side of the road leading from Jericho toward Jerusalem, the two blind men listened to
the passing crowd, headed toward the Passover feast.
Hearing that the Rabbi Jesus was in the crowd, the
two men cried out, loudly and continuously, "Have
mercy on us, Son of David." As was the custom

in those days, as a rabbi walked along, he would teach, and the crowd would listen to his teaching. The crowd attempted to silence the two men who were disturbing the ability of the crowd to hear Jesus as they walked. But the two refused to be quieted, and Jesus turned and asked them, as we see him so frequently do, "What do you want?" The two asked that their eyes be opened, and when Jesus healed them, they immediately followed him.

Two insistent blind men. An annoyed crowd. A direct question from Jesus. A clear response.

Healing and restoration.

INTERRUPTIONS TO JESUS' TEACHING often are powerful. The interrupter may act as the counterpoint to Jesus' teaching, the voice of Everyman raising a common concern of listeners or voicing a point of view that Jesus wanted to address. The immediate interrupting the important — this is how our days go. Sometimes we tersely turn aside the demand: "If you knew how important this task is, you wouldn't interrupt," we think. Sometimes we deal with the interruption with much sighing and impatience. We barely tolerate the endless parade of telemarketers who interrupt our dinners, our conversations, our story times with our children with their shrill demands to buy their product or service.

And so we may side with the crowd: "Be quiet,

beggars; I'm listening to the Master! We're talking eternity talk here!" But these two men interrupted the Master because they believed, believed entirely, that Jesus could give them their sight back, and nothing, *nothing*, was so important that it could silence their cry for healing from the one they believed could give it. How eagerly do we want our pain healed, how fervently are we willing to chase after the Master to be healed, how strongly do we believe that Jesus is the one who can answer our prayers? This is a faith of passion, of urgency, of intensity, not a faith of politeness, of the quiet, halfhearted, tentative question. It is a faith that requires us to know with an honest clarity that which needs Jesus' touch. How would we answer if Jesus turned to us and said, "What do you want?" When faced with his gaze, a gaze that must indeed have pierced the soul, seeking and finding the most basic, most real part of ourselves, how would we answer?

> *God, help us to want your touch in our lives*
> *so much that we will seek you out*
> *with intensity and faith.*

James and John

Matthew 20:17–24

And as Jesus was going up to Jerusalem, he took the twelve disciples aside, and on the way he said to them, "Behold, we are going up to Jerusalem; and the Son of man will be delivered to the chief priests and scribes, and they will condemn him to death, and deliver him to the Gentiles to be mocked and scourged and crucified, and he will be raised on the third day."

Then the mother of the sons of Zebedee came up to him, with her sons, and kneeling before him she asked him for something. And he said to her, "What do you want?" She said to him, "Command that these two sons of mine may sit, one at your right hand and one at your left, in your kingdom." But Jesus answered, "You do not know what you are asking. Are you able to drink the cup that I am to drink?" They said to him, "We are able." He said to them, "You will drink my cup, but to sit at my right hand and at my left is not mine to grant, but it is for those for whom it has been prepared by my Father." And when the ten heard it, they were indignant at the two brothers.

Mark 10:35–45

And James and John, the sons of Zebedee, came forward to him, and said to him, "Teacher, we want you to do for us whatever we ask of you." And he said to them, "What do you want me to do for you?" And they said to him, "Grant us to sit, one at your right hand and one at your left, in your glory." But Jesus said to them, "You do not know what you are asking. Are you able to drink the cup that I drink, or to be baptized with the baptism with which I am baptized?" And they said to him, "We are able." And Jesus said to them, "The cup that I drink you will drink; and with the baptism with which I am baptized, you will be baptized; but to sit at my right hand or at my left is not mine to grant, but it is for those for whom it has been prepared." And when the ten heard it, they began to be indignant at James and John. And Jesus called them to him and said to them, "You know that those who are supposed to rule over the

Gentiles lord it over them, and their great men exercise authority over them. But it shall not be so among you; but whoever would be great among you must be your servant, and whoever would be first among you must be slave of all. For the Son of man also came not to be served but to serve, and to give his life as a ransom for many."

Both Matthew and Mark tell the story of a request to Jesus that he promise to elevate James and John, the sons of Zebedee and possibly the cousins of Jesus, to positions of power in Jesus' kingdom. In Matthew, the request is reported as being made by the mother of the two. In response to the request, Jesus asks the two brothers if they are able to drink of the same cup that he is to drink, or be willing to pay the same price for following God. (Christian tradition and Scripture has it that James was in fact one of the first martyrs of the faith, while John lived to the age of a hundred or more.[4]) In Luke 22:24, we read that even during the Last Supper, the disciples were arguing among themselves which one was the greatest. In each case, Jesus' response deals in one way or another with the cost and the meaning of greatness.

The constant themes among these stories are that "greatness" is measured among Christians on a scale that is different from that used in the rest of the world and that there is a cost to following Christ. Greatness among Christians is not to be measured by wealth or power, but by service. The price of the Christian life may be sharp and dramatic as it was with James, or it might be exacted over the course of a whole life as it was with John, a life of daily challenges to follow Christ, daily temptations to choose another road.

WE ARE OFTEN TOLD THAT WHEN FACED with a situation involving choice, we should ask ourselves, "What would Jesus do?" Yet, much of following Jesus is finding another way — not just picking between two clearly defined paths, but finding a third path, one we didn't even know was there. Often questions posed to Jesus presented two choices, and the inquirer asked, "Which way should we go?" Frequently, Jesus' answer opened up a whole new way of thinking, one altogether unanticipated.

So it is with Jesus' consideration of what it means to be great; the disciples clearly thought that greatness was measured by what was gained in life, such as wealth or power. In contrast, the Christian measure of greatness is what you have given. Did you give with arms open wide to hold all the world and its hurt, were your fingers spread apart to let your resources flow through unfettered to bring water to the desert, food to the hungry, comfort to the sore at heart? Did you fling open your doors to those who need to understand the warmth of home and the security of family? Did you give of yourself to those who had never received positive, personal, encouraging attention? Did you use your gifts and share your skills to lift up, or did you clutch all these to yourself?

As adults, we all learn there is a price to be paid for most of our choices in life, even if the only price is being able to select only our first choice and having to forego our second choice. The cost of discipleship, well, that is what we are afraid of, is it not? We imagine God asking us to forfeit family, comfort, and security, and we fear, deeply fear, being asked to do so.

> *Help us, Lord,*
> *to learn to see choices with your eyes,*
> *and to trust you enough to follow you*
> *on the path of discipleship.*

Martha of Bethany

John 11:1–5, 17–27, 38–40

Now a certain man was ill, Lazarus of Bethany, the village of Mary and her sister Martha. It was Mary who anointed the Lord with ointment and wiped his feet with her hair, whose brother Lazarus was ill. So the sisters sent to him, saying, "Lord, he whom you love is ill." But when Jesus heard it he said, "This illness is not unto death; it is for the glory of God, so that the Son of God may be glorified by means of it."

Now Jesus loved Martha and her sister and Lazarus. . . .

Now when Jesus came, he found that Lazarus had already been in the tomb four days. Bethany was near Jerusalem, about two miles off, and many of the Jews had come to Martha and Mary to console them concerning their brother. When Martha heard that Jesus was coming, she went and met him, while Mary sat in the house. Martha said to Jesus, "Lord, if you had been here, my brother would not have died. And even now, I know that whatever you ask from God, God will give you." Jesus said to her, "Your brother will rise again." Martha said to him, "I know that he will rise again in the resurrection at the last day." Jesus said to her, "I am the resurrection and the life; he who believes in me, though he die, yet shall he live, and whoever lives and believes in me shall never die. Do you believe this?" She said to him, "Yes, Lord; I believe that you are the Christ, the Son of God, he who is coming into the world." . . .

Then Jesus, deeply moved again, came to the tomb; it was a cave, and a stone lay upon it. Jesus said, "Take away the stone." Martha, the sister of the dead man, said to him, "Lord, by this time there will be an odor, for he has been dead four days." Jesus said to her, "Did I not tell you that if you would believe you would see the glory of God?"

Martha is so easy to picture, we almost fall into stereotype. We see her big capable hands, able to do any household task before her. We see her lack of finesse, her directness, her straightforwardness. We see her putting aside anything she might want to do in order to do what duty compels her to do or habit requires her to do. She would be generous with what she has, her skills, her home, her cooking. And yet, she would also probably keep score, check whether others were doing what they ought to be doing. A favor given was a favor that should be returned. Obligations attached to friendship. Loyalty counted. Martha was one for whom friendships were a back-door, across-the-fence sort of thing. One where you could count on everyone being where they should be, following a known routine every day. Where friends were there when you needed them, just as you were there for them. Her desire for predictability and her devotion to duty warred with her love for Jesus, who showed up at odd times, occasional moments, without much warning. Even so, there were hidden depths of passion, of intensity in Martha, that could spill out unchecked.

And so, when her brother Lazarus died, perhaps after she had nursed and cared for him for months, the pent-up frustration and grief and resentment of harbored thoughts bursts out. "Lord, if you had been here, you could have saved him!" she accuses. Yet, Martha's initial outburst is followed by such a clear statement of faith in Jesus, such a solid affirmation of Jesus as the Messiah, that we watch her faith in what Jesus can do and be literally grow in front of our eyes. But when Jesus proposes to roll back the stone in front of the tomb, it is practical Martha who cautions about the odor of a four-day-old corpse. The practical, the present, the knowable jousting with the possible, the miracle, the faith-filled moment.

W E CAN LEARN A LOT FROM MARTHA. We all settle into routines as we grow older. Amid the chaos and unpredictability of the rest of the world, we want our homes and our lives to be havens of peace and order. Moreover, there are parts of our lives we don't want to have to think about, that we want to keep sacrosanct, that we should be allowed to have untouched and unchallenged. But with Jesus, that doesn't always happen. When we follow Jesus, when we truly make our lives his, our time his, our homes his, then things happen, things change. We are shaken out of our routines, our predictable ways of doing things. Our time gets given to people and causes we would not have thought before to have chosen. We find ourselves open to ideas and demands and ways of giving of ourselves and our resources that those who do not follow Jesus do not understand. And always, we learn to temper our knowledge of the practical with the faith that the impossible may become reality.

> *Lord, help us, like Martha,*
> *to rush forward headlong to meet you,*
> *to know that you are our salvation,*
> *that anything with you is possible.*

Even when we would hold ourselves back,
let us learn that there are no facts,
no "realities" big enough
to stop the work of your will.

Lazarus

John 12:1, 9–11

Six days before the Passover, Jesus came to Bethany, where Lazarus was, whom Jesus had raised from the dead....

When the great crowd of the Jews learned that he was there, they came, not only on account of Jesus but also to see Lazarus, whom he had raised from the dead. So the chief priests planned to put Lazarus also to death, because on account of him many of the Jews were going away and believing in Jesus.

When someone we love is seriously ill, perhaps dying, the world narrows down to that face, that hospital bed, what the doctor says. We look at the body of our beloved, and in some ways it perplexes us, for it seems no different than it was yesterday; the same parts are there, the same face, and yet, and yet, the presence of illness pervades all. We are aware that inside that sometimes tough, sometimes fragile shell of skin and muscles and bone, a war is being waged by microbes and cells and invidious creeping invaders. The energy of life fades or slows, the face sinks, the effort to move becomes draining. We look up and see as if in a slow motion movie, the nurses moving about, people walking along the sidewalk below, and we wonder how life has continued. Shouldn't the whole world be focused on this room, this bed, this person? How does life go on when mine has slowed to a crawl?

But, oh, the wondrous sense of release when life comes surging back, when the forces of energy return and the world opens wide and free again. Everything is intensified; where once there was only a gray fog, now we see intensely. The snap of the cold winter air against our skin, the riot of a fiery sunset reminds us of life and the ability to sense, something we now welcome. The preciousness of life and the glory of living now seem riches enough.

WE ALL KNOW THE STORY OF LAZARUS, the friend whom Jesus raised from the dead. We often struggle with the fact of raising the dead, our morbid curiosity wondering what Lazarus would have looked like, been like. Our minds focus on his sisters, Mary and Martha, but we skitter away from Lazarus. We know that Lazarus, Mary, and Martha were close friends and frequent hosts of Jesus in their home in Bethany. We do know that Lazarus was ill, died, and was raised by Jesus. But the release back into life for Lazarus, as well as for his loving sisters, Martha and Mary, was followed, oh, so closely, by the death of their dearest friend, Jesus. Did they believe God could resurrect him just as Jesus had raised Lazarus? When Lazarus was given a second chance at life, was he a different man? Did he see and feel and experience differently?

After Lazarus was returned to life, we know that he was such an effective and compelling witness for Jesus that the religious authorities wanted to put him to death as well. Perhaps Lazarus tells us that what holds us back is fear — unspoken fears of loss and pain and death — and that once those fears are replaced by trust, we can do anything. In Jesus, we see a demonstration of what life can be like when we are not hampered by fear.

God, help us live every day as a precious gift.
Help us to know
that when our hope seems gone
you are the everlasting source
of all hope, all life, all power.
And when a life does draw to a close,
let us rejoice in the return of the beloved to you.
But most of all, help us to put aside fear,
to become compelling witnesses

for a life lived with you
because we know that joy waits for us
on the other side,
a release into the very presence
of the Most High!

Mary of Bethany

John 12:1–8

Six days before the Passover, Jesus came to Bethany, where Lazarus was, whom Jesus had raised from the dead. There they made him a supper; Martha served, and Lazarus was one of those at table with him. Mary took a pound of costly ointment of pure nard and anointed the feet of Jesus and wiped his feet with her hair; and the house was filled with the fragrance of the ointment. But Judas Iscariot, one of his disciples (he who was to betray him), said, "Why was this ointment not sold for three hundred denarii and given to the poor?" This he said, not that he cared for the poor but because he was a thief, and as he had the money box he used to take what was put into it. Jesus said, "Let her alone, let her keep it for the day of my burial. The poor you always have with you, but you do not always have me."

It is the evening meal in the home of Martha, Mary, and Lazarus in Bethany, the night before Jesus' triumphal Palm Sunday entry into Jerusalem. Bethany, which was only two miles from Jerusalem and was an officially acceptable place for Passover pilgrims to stay, would have been teeming with new arrivals. Jesus, the disciples, and perhaps other guests are eating supper, which Martha, predictably, serves. While Jesus alone may be aware of the events that will be unfolding over the next several days, the disciples possess a certain wariness, revealed earlier in John 11:8 when Jesus announces he is going to return to Bethany now that Lazarus has died. The disciples say in astonishment and deep concern, "But, Rabbi, the Jews were just seeking to stone you and yet you would return there again?" The disciples may have been looking over their shoulder throughout the day, anxiously watching for the grasped sword, the raised stone, the march of the temple police.

The evening assumes a new character, though, when lit by the light of unlimited love. Mary enters the room, carrying a box of costly nard, usually used to care for a body prior to burial. She tenderly, slowly, begins to care for Jesus as if no one else were in the room, not anointing his head, but his feet, the workaday, callused, road-roughened feet of a traveler. Looking about almost absent-mindedly for a towel to wipe his feet with, and seeing none (for she had not planned this in detail in advance), she stupefies all in the room as she slowly reaches without thinking for the nearest useful tool, her hair. She cannot seem to break the spell-binding scene to get up for a towel and then come back. Transfixed, we watch as Mary lingers over her task, in a quiet, even drawn-out, peaceful contrast to the whirl of coming events. We smell the sweet scent of the fragrant nard fill the house. We see Jesus, alert but accepting, unafraid of this demonstration of all-encompassing love from Mary. And then, perhaps, satisfied that she has done what love moved her to do, she looks up solemnly to search Jesus' face, sees quiet approval and warm acceptance, and then silently glides out of the room, her face glowing.

M UCH HAS BEEN WRITTEN of the reactions of others in the room, the calculation of the value of love's gift as being sufficient to feed five thousand people. Yet, what we see in Mary is the gift of true love — the ability to give without counting the cost, to give all that one has and still count the gift insufficient. We don't often think of giving gifts to the adult Jesus; rather, it is easier for us to bring gifts to the baby in the manger. We have trouble imagining what gift we could give to the adult Jesus, the Jesus who understands with compassionate accuracy the heart that gives the gift. Mary gave because she needed to give and because she knew in her heart, in a way she may not have even understood, that Jesus needed to be anointed in this way. What gift can we bring to the Jesus who is headed for the cross, to die for us?

> *Lord, help us to give Jesus*
> *nothing less than ourselves,*
> *to pour out all that we have*
> *until we see that the more we give,*
> *the more we have to give.*

The Owner of the Ass and the Colt

Matthew 21:1–7

And when they drew near to Jerusalem and came to Bethphage, to the Mount of Olives, then Jesus sent two disciples, saying to them, "Go into the village opposite you, and immediately you will find an ass tied, and a colt with her; untie them and bring them to me. If any one says anything to you, you shall say, 'The Lord has need of them,' and he will send them immediately." This took place to fulfill what was spoken by the prophet, saying,

> *"Tell the daughter of Zion,*
> *Behold your king is coming to you,*
> *humble, and mounted on an ass,*
> *and on a colt, the foal of an ass."*

The disciples went and did as Jesus had directed them; they brought the ass and the colt, and put their garments on them, and he sat thereon.

On the road to Jerusalem, the disciples and Jesus came to Bethphage, to the Mount of Olives, where Jesus sent out two disciples and directed them to the village where he said they would immediately find an ass and a colt. They were to take the two animals without seeking out the owner, although if asked, they were to use a code phrase: "The Lord has need of them." Everything happened as Jesus directed. Clearly, Jesus or some of his followers had established in advance that the animals would be available to Jesus and had determined a code phrase, so that all would be ready when the time came.

Who was the owner of the ass and the colt? How did Jesus come to know that the person owned the specific animals he needed? How did they come to an arrangement that Jesus could have them? Perhaps Jesus encountered the owner watering or feeding his animals. Perhaps the owner had heard Jesus preach and afterward had come and said, "You know, if you ever need anything, just let me know.... " Perhaps the owner asked no questions, but just bowed reverently and acquiesced to this request of the man of God. Most likely, the animals were owned by a close friend of Jesus.

In the nineteenth century, it was said that when Queen Mary of England visited a home and expressed specific admiration for a particular *objet d'art,* it was considered to be subtle request that the owner send the item around to the palace within a few days as a "gift."[5] It is unlikely, however, that this was the sort of subtle coercion that provided the animals for Jesus at the required time.

BUT WHAT IF, WHEN ASKED, the owner had said, "Well, Jesus, I don't really want to give up that ass and colt. I can sell them in the market for a pretty good price. Why don't you take this older fella over here — he'll last that short ride you have in mind." If God were to ask us for something very specific, how would we react? If God asked us to be in a certain place or talk to a certain person or make some particular sacrifice, how would we react? We usually want to be in control; we decide how much of our money we will give back to the church, or what activities we will support. We want to give to God, but we want to retain the control over what, when, and at what cost to us. We want to pray to God specifically, but we don't necessarily want to listen to God specifically.

Hearing God specifically rather than generally demands the closeness of a relationship between God and ourselves that is maintained through constant communication, constant prayer, or talking to God throughout the big and small times of our lives. What do we cling to so closely that if God asked us, we would hesitate or refuse to give it up? How much do

we really trust God to know that if he asks for a sacrifice on our part, a specific sacrifice, there is some
higher good involved?

God, help us to hear you specifically.
Help us to grow
in the communication we have with you
until the very minutes of each day
are suffused and filled
with an understanding of and a trust in you.

The Crowd on Palm Sunday

Matthew 21:1–11

And when they drew near to Jerusalem and came to Bethphage, to the Mount of Olives, then Jesus sent two disciples, saying to them, "Go into the village opposite you, and immediately you will find an ass tied, and a colt with her; untie them and bring them to me. If any one says anything to you, you shall say, 'The Lord has need of them,' and he will send them immediately." This took place to fulfill what was spoken by the prophet, saying,

> *"Tell the daughter of Zion,*
> *Behold your king is coming to you,*
> *humble, and mounted on an ass,*
> *and on a colt, the foal of an ass."*

The disciples went and did as Jesus had directed them; they brought the ass and the colt, and put their garments on them, and he sat thereon. Most of the crowd spread their garments on the

*road, and others cut branches from the trees and
spread them on the road. And the crowds that
went before him and that followed him shouted,
"Hosanna to the Son of David! Blessed is he
who comes in the name of the Lord! Hosanna
in the highest!" And when he entered Jerusalem,
all the city was stirred, saying, "Who is this?"
And the crowds said, "This is the prophet Jesus
from Nazareth of Galilee."*

Much has been written about the kind of Messiah
that the Jews expected, wanted, hoped for, longed
for: a kingly Messiah, one who would smash all the
enemies of Israel into oblivion, prove the superiority
of the followers of the Law, a sort of grand vindica-
tor, one who would pay back all of Israel's collective
and personal enemies for all the insults, injustices,
wrongs, tragedies, and horrors that had been inflicted
on the people of God over the years. A king of un-
equaled might and power. A sort of national warrior
king/hero. All the energy of this Messiah would be
directed outward, not inward.

This was the expectation that the people had, and
it was that expectation that they honored when Jesus
rode in on a donkey to Jerusalem on what we call
Palm Sunday. Perhaps some knew and understood
the symbolism of Jesus riding on an ass, a symbol
of a king who came in peace, rather than riding in

on a horse, which would have symbolized a conquering king. Others may have heard of the rabbi from Galilee and had come to see who this newest charismatic preacher was. Others may have been caught up, swept along with the thrill of waving palm fronds at a feast time, throwing cloaks down on the ground for this young rabbi to ride on, being part of something unusual that would make a great story to tell the relatives newly arrived from out of town.

THE JESUS THEY HONORED and the Jesus who arrived were not the same. The crowd honored their own expectations and saw in Jesus only that which fulfilled their hopes. They did not "see" or understand the Jesus before them. How well, how clearly do we see Jesus? We return to favorite passages or parables or sayings of his, and leave the more difficult ones for another day. We see the Jesus we want to see, the one who reflects what sort of a "Messiah" we think would fix whatever ills we see in the world, straighten out the wrong thinking of whomever we disagree with. In many ways, we are no different from the crowd on Palm Sunday, remaking Jesus into the great defender of our personal faith, our personal beliefs. We do not want to be challenged or forced to rethink our lives or the way we follow Jesus. We always find a way to make Jesus agree with our point of view.

We read that Jesus wept over the misunderstanding populace of Jerusalem, a populace that welcomed him in cheering throngs — and in jeering crowds later put him to death. Does he weep for us? He rode into a city where the Lord's temple was the site of corrupt businesses, where the religious leaders were more interested in self-righteous aggrandizement than in serving God and those in need. Does Jesus come into our lives, and what does he see when he looks? How often do we really see Jesus and what do we see when we do?

God, help us to see Jesus on your terms, not ours,
with an understanding you have given us
rather than a belief in an image
we have forced upon you.

The Greek Pilgrims

John 12:20–22

Now among those who went up to worship at the feast were some Greeks. So these came to Philip, who was from Bethsaida in Galilee, and said to him, "Sir, we wish to see Jesus." Philip went and told Andrew; Andrew went with Philip and they told Jesus.

The Greeks were known throughout the ancient world as travelers and as seekers of truth. So it was not unusual to see that there were Greeks who came to Jerusalem for the Passover, perhaps to see the largest feast of the Jewish year, or to see the famous temple. Perhaps these Greeks even were believers in the one God. Some have conjectured that perhaps these Greek pilgrims had been present when Jesus cleansed the Court of the Gentiles, the only part of the temple precincts where non-Jews were allowed. The Greeks then sought out Philip, a disciple of Jesus with a Greek name, to get an audience with Jesus.

They had heard of Jesus since their arrival in Jerusalem. Perhaps they saw his compelling and transfixing actions or heard him teach, and they desired to talk with him personally.

But we see that Philip didn't quite know what to do. The disciples had kept children away from Jesus, only to have Jesus want them to be allowed in. Perhaps at one time they had also thought that Jesus' meeting with the powerful scribes and Pharisees was a good idea, but that had since proved to be disastrous. So Philip was no longer sure of the right sort of people to bring to Jesus. As a result, he asked Andrew what to do. We read in John 6:8–9 about a telling incident that showed that Andrew was the disciple who knew how to reach people. In this account of the feeding of the crowd of five thousand people, Andrew was the one who knew that a small boy in such a mass of humanity had five barley loaves and two fishes, and he took him to Jesus to provide the stuff of which miracles are made. Of all the disciples, Andrew had the ability to relate at a personal, open level.[6] And Andrew knew what to do: take the Greek pilgrims to Jesus.

From this introduction came Jesus' speech on glory, eternal life, and service. John does not relate the story of Jesus in the Garden of Gethsemane; rather, John places Jesus here, troubled over what is about to happen, and includes the voice of God speaking to Jesus in front of the Greeks. This is the first hint that appears, with the presence of Gentiles at this key moment, that the Gospel message is for Jews and Gentiles alike. The Good News is for everyone!

W HEN WE PONDER THIS STORY, there are several ways to find an entry point. Are we like Philip, unsure of how to bring others to Jesus and no longer sure of our ability to just tell of our faith? Or are we like Andrew, seeing people where they are and understanding that all they need is a guide to point the way and Jesus will do the rest? Or are we like the Greeks? We are not told what happened to the Greeks, and most likely the disciples didn't know. The Greeks came, perhaps seeking truth; they saw and heard Jesus, and then disappeared from view. If nothing changed for the Greeks, then we think of those who come, listen, and do not absorb. In the marketplace of philosophies, there are those who dabble, taste, try, but have no intention of commitment. If the Greeks did believe, then we think of our own role as disciples: we are responsible for sowing, planting, watering, and nurturing, but the harvesting is in God's hands.

> *God, help us to be willing guideposts,*
> *willing introducers to Jesus.*
> *Help us to trust that you will speak*
> *to the hearts of honest seekers.*

The Temple Sellers

Matthew 21:12–13

> *And Jesus entered the temple of God and drove out all who sold and bought in the temple, and he overturned the tables of the money-changers and the seats of those who sold pigeons. He said to them, "It is written, 'My house shall be called a house of prayer'; but you make it a den of robbers."*

The Palm Sunday procession took Jesus straight to the temple in Jerusalem, where he continued his dramatic symbolic actions. Matthew says that Jesus drove out all who bought and sold in the temple and that he overturned the tables of the moneychangers and the seats of those who sold pigeons. His accusations and his actions are strong. "You have made this temple a den of robbers!" We see an angry Jesus, a righteous Jesus, a Jesus of action and power and determination. A Jesus willing to take on the powers that be, driving out those who must have engaged in their slimy practices with the assent of those who governed the temple. For one who wanted to come in and become part of the ruling structure of Jerusalem, it would be a disastrous start. But for one who took the temple seriously, who believed in the temple as a representation of God, any act that diminished the holiness of the temple in any way would require rebuke.

Who were these sellers and moneychangers and what role did they play? All Jews were required to pay a certain "temple tax" each year at the Passover time, either in local currency at a local booth during a prescribed period or, later, in a special currency at the temple, where most foreign pilgrims paid the tax. The moneychangers changed foreign currency into the accepted currency, usually tacking on a service fee for both changing the money and for giving change back. Likewise, the unblemished animal required for any temple sacrifice could be bought outside the temple grounds, but the priest could reject the offered animal and require that a new animal be bought inside the temple, usually at many times the "outside the temple" price. Thus, a vested interest, an accepted way of doing business, built up between the temple priests and those who provided the necessary services to those who came to worship, perhaps earning exorbitant profits as a result.

HOW DO WE RELATE TO THE MONEYCHANGERS and the vendors of sacrificial animals? What in their story speaks to us? Perhaps we can imagine a similar reaction from Jesus every time we take something intended for our good and corrupt it, use it in a way that fails to honor that purpose for which God gave it to us. When we trample on the feelings of others, when we abuse our bodies, when we misuse the gifts of nature, when we fail to use the talents and gifts we have been given for God's kingdom, then we are like those who exploit but do not honor what God has given us. Perhaps we also act like the moneychangers and the vendors when we keep away those who approach God through our unwillingness to accept differences, through our barriers that require conformity to our ways, our style, or our beliefs in order to be part of *our* family of God.

Help us, God, to see where our actions
are keeping pilgrims and seekers away from you.
Help us to look at our own actions
in the light of your righteous indignation.
In what ways are we supporting
those who subvert your will?

The Widow Who Gave a Mite

Mark 12:41–44

And he sat down opposite the treasury, and watched the multitude putting money into the treasury. Many rich people put in large sums. And a poor widow came, and put in two copper coins, which make a penny. And he called his disciples to him, and said to them, "Truly, I say to you, this poor widow has put in more than all those who are contributing to the treasury. For they all contributed out of their abundance; but she out of her poverty has put in everything she had, her whole living."

There were thirteen collecting boxes, each for a different purpose related to the upkeep and maintenance of the temple, in the Court of the Women in the temple. Those who gave would put their offerings in these trumpet-shaped boxes, often throwing them in with enough force to make a loud noise as their contribution clattered down the funnel of the trumpet, the coins chasing each other down into the offering box. The larger the coins, the louder the sound. Those who gave greatly thus brought attention to themselves, as those surrounding would look and see who gave so generously. The gift alone was not enough for some; the need for recognition was equally great.

We read that during this last week of Jesus' life, after he cleansed the temple precincts of those who would steal from the reverence of the temple, Jesus sat down to watch the crowds. Into his line of sight came a widow, one of no particular standing or presence. This widow was impoverished, her offering of two of the smallest coins in the realm barely making a sound as they rolled down the tube — yet Jesus heard them. Her gift of two copper coins pales in significance beside the gift of the costly nard of Mary of Bethany, but Jesus praises them both, for he looks beyond the gift to the heart. The widow gave her whole living, her whole hedge against abject poverty. All, Jesus says, she gave all. And as small as her coins were, in the economy of God's kingdom, her gift was greater than all the rest.

WHAT COMFORT JESUS MUST HAVE TAKEN from watching this event! To see that there still were faithful believers, who quietly and fervently followed their faith, who lived lives of sacrifice and discipline in order to carry out the dictates of their beliefs. After days and even years of struggling with the religious authorities who split every hair, who argued over every action, who looked for barriers in the Law to doing good works, how refreshing, how restoring for Jesus to see one for whom God was all that was important, for whom faith was not a game or a political power struggle for control. The widow and her sacrificial gift restored perspective to Jesus. Further, the widow gave of what she had, without holding anything back. She gave until it cost.

What in our lives is it that we refuse to give, because it will cost us in a way we don't want to pay? Is it our time, our selves, our personal insights? Do we refuse to crack our facade and share what we have learned about life and faith with others, hoarding our faith as it were and sharing it with none? Do we give money instead of our hands and heart? Do we give our best to others but our worst to our families? Are we unwilling to give up certain habits, certain patterns, certain rituals, like watching television or a hobby or a sport, that spare us from having to be involved more personally with those around us? What do we refuse to give because it costs too much?

Lord, give us the faith
to give what we have,
not what we can spare.

Priests, Scribes, and Pharisees

Matthew 22:15, 34–35

Then the Pharisees went and took counsel how to entangle him in his talk....

But when the Pharisees heard that he had silenced the Sadducees, they came together. And one of them, a lawyer, asked him a question, to test him.

Matthew 23:1–7

Then said Jesus to the crowds and to his disciples, "The scribes and the Pharisees sit on Moses' seat; so practice and observe whatever they tell you, but not what they do; for they preach, but do not practice. They bind heavy burdens, hard to bear, and lay them on men's shoulders; but they themselves will not move them with their finger. They do all their deeds to be seen by men; for they make their phylacteries broad and their fringes long, and they love the place of honor at feasts and the best seats in the synagogues, and salutations in the market places, and being called rabbi by men."

The Pharisees were a group of extremely devout lay people who had dedicated themselves to following every minute detail of the Law — and making sure that every one around them knew that they were doing so. In contrast, the Sadducees, who did not believe in life after death, were more aristocratic and tended to hold positions of political prominence. The high priest was usually a Sadducee. Like a venomous Greek chorus, we see the scribes (lawyers), the Pharisees, the Sadducees, the chief priests, and the elders follow Jesus from Bethany to Jerusalem, appearing at his trial before Pontius Pilate and again before Herod. Even at the foot of the cross, we see this same group taunting Jesus; amazingly, this same group that had seen Lazarus raised from the dead said to Jesus that if only he would step down from the cross, *then* they would believe. We see them everywhere, planning arcane questions of the Law, asking Jesus leading questions designed to cause him to either look foolish in front of the people or to in some way appear to be rebellious against Roman rule. We read that throughout the Passion week they plotted ways to arrest Jesus, to hunt him down, to charge him, and to ensure his death. At every point, we see Jesus confounding them, often tossing back to them a question for which they could not find a politically acceptable answer, one that would not place themselves in the wrong.

Despite all their careful scripting of these encounters, they nonetheless always managed to lose whatever battle of wits or logic or faith they had planned. So, they seem to us sort of like a religious perpetual motion machine: they just keep coming and coming. It is almost a relief to see Jesus come out swinging in Matthew 23:13–35, to really let loose with the scribes and Pharisees, to expose all their petty hypocrisy. It was this group, after all, that was plotting to kill one of their fellow Jews, while at the same time they carefully tithed the herbs that grew in a kitchen pot. It is a faith of inconsequentials, one that ignores the higher purpose behind the Law. Seven times Jesus denounces their hypocrisy with passionate conviction, yet underlying it all is a sort of sadness, for this way of following the Law was surely not what God had in mind when he first gave the Ten Commandments to Moses.

WE DON'T LIKE THE SCRIBES AND PHARISEES. We do not see their faith; we see only their assumed piety. We do not see a driving love for God; we see only a burning hatred for one who spoke with the authority of God. When we become consumed with the smallest detail of church operations or functioning, when we spend our energy feuding over the specific ways of following our faith, are we becoming like the Pharisees and absorbing ourselves in the smaller rather than the larger matters of faith? When we ensure that others know what we have contributed to the church, are we parading our faith like the Pharisees?

Help us, Lord, to search out the ways
in which we are trivializing you,
losing you in the details,
substituting focus on the tiniest things in order
to protect us from facing the larger issues of faith.

Owner of the Upper Room

Luke 22:7–13

Then came the day of Unleavened Bread, on which the passover lamb had to be sacrificed. So Jesus sent Peter and John, saying, "Go and prepare the passover for us, that we may eat it." They said to him, "Where will you have us prepare it?" He said to them, "Behold, when you have entered the city, a man carrying a jar of water will meet you; follow him into the house which he enters, and tell the householder, 'The Teacher says to you, Where is the guest room, where I am to eat the passover with my disciples?' And he will show you a large upper room furnished; there make ready." And they went, and found it as he had told them; and they prepared the passover.

Just as Jesus had arranged in advance to have the ass and the colt ready for his dramatic entry into Jerusalem, so he had also arranged for a place to have the

Passover meal. Peter and John are sent ahead into the city to look for an unusual sight, that of a man carrying a jug of water, a task usually reserved for women. This man would then lead them to the house where the upper room had been set aside for Jesus' use. Jewish tradition required that the Paschal lamb be shared by at least a group of ten, making Passover a time of communal feasting.

We do not read that the owner of the home was one of the disciples, although several commentators have conjectured that the home belonged to Mary, mother of John Mark. It may be that the owner of the home had left his or her house and was celebrating the Passover meal with another group. Hosting Jesus would be an honor, one that a host would want to tell friends about, showing connections to this well-known rabbi. And yet, it would appear that the feast was held in relative secrecy, requiring passwords and apparently the absence of the servants of the home.

After the crucifixion, we read that the disciples stayed in a room where the door was barred for fear of the Jewish authorities. Luke, writing in the book of Acts, has the disciples returning to an upper room, which tradition seems to hold as being the same upper room where the Last Supper was held. If so, the owner of the house was not only a generous person, but a brave person, for to harbor the disciples at that time might have been very dangerous indeed.

THROUGHOUT THE GOSPELS is a plethora of people without names, whose acts supported, undergirded, and provided the means for Jesus' ministry. We find throughout the Passion story alone the unnamed owners of the ass and the colt, the unnamed owner of the Garden of Gethsemene, the unnamed owner of the upper room. The women who followed Jesus along the path to Golgotha and many of the women at the foot of the cross have no names. In our study of the Bible, we tend to spend most of our time on those who have a name, as if that gives their stories greater importance. In our own lives, we wonder rhetorically if anyone will know our name even thirty years after our death. However, what matters is that these generous souls were present, they provided what was needed, and Jesus knew their names. They asked for nothing more than the opportunity to serve one in whom they believed. That takes a big person.

How important to us is recognition for our good works? Do we get disgruntled if we are not among those thanked at the end of a major effort? Do we need to see our name in the publications and the honor rolls? Can we give without credit, give what we have to God without needing to get recognition, without even knowing the final result?

God, help us to understand
that we have been called
to plant without seeing the harvest,
to water where others have sown,
to bring others' seedlings to fruition.
For we know that now we see in part,
but then we shall know fully.

Jesus at
the Last Supper

John 13:1–9, 12–17

Now before the feast of the Passover, when Jesus knew that his hour had come to depart out of this world to the Father, having loved his own who were in the world, he loved them to the end. And during supper, when the devil had already put it into the heart of Judas Iscariot, Simon's son, to betray him, Jesus, knowing that the Father had given all things into his hands, and that he had come from God and was going to God, rose from supper, laid aside his garments, and girded himself with a towel. Then he poured water into a basin, and began to wash the disciples' feet, and to wipe them with the towel with which he was girded. He came to Simon Peter; and Peter said to him, "Lord, do you wash my feet?" Jesus answered him, "What I am doing you do not know now, but afterward

*you will understand." Peter said to him, "You
shall never wash my feet." Jesus answered him,
"If I do not wash you, you have no part in me."
Simon Peter said to him, "Lord, not my feet
only but also my hands and my head!" . . .*

*When he had washed their feet, and taken
his garments, and resumed his place, he said
to them, "Do you know what I have done to
you? You call me Teacher and Lord; and you
are right, for so I am. If I then, your Lord and
Teacher, have washed your feet, you also ought
to wash one another's feet. For I have given you
an example, that you also should do as I have
done to you. Truly, truly, I say to you, a servant is not greater than his master; nor is he
who is sent greater than he who sent him. If
you know these things, blessed are you if you
do them. . . . "*

When we think of all the expectations the disciples
might still have held regarding the Messiah, they
surely had no thought that the deliverer of Israel
would stoop to assume the task of a servant, washing
the dirt of the road off his followers' feet. Normally,
there would have been a large water pot at the front
door of a house and a servant to wash a visitor's feet.
Perhaps none of the disciples had seen to these ar-
rangements, or perhaps the owner of the home had

not left a servant behind to perform this courtesy, assuming that Jesus would have someone to do this service for him and his followers. Just as they had earlier disputed among themselves who was greatest, perhaps none of them was willing to perform this menial task for the others. To our modern eyes, it may also seem strange that people just didn't wash their own feet and leave it at that.

Imagine the reactions of the disciples as they understood what Jesus intended to do. At first, shuffling their feet, glancing at each other, shrugging, as if to indicate this was another act of Jesus they just didn't get. Simon Peter bursts out what they all may have been thinking, "Not my feet, Master! You shall never wash my feet!" When Jesus tells Peter that if he does not wash his feet, Peter would have no part of him, then the room grows silent. Suddenly shy, they are unable to look at each other as they wait his slow movement toward them. Jesus even extended his ministrations to Judas, who Jesus already knew would betray him. Even the guilty, even the betrayers, are included in Jesus' serving love. Jesus emphasized the concept of servanthood and servant leadership during the last week of his life, perhaps providing a way for his followers to understand all that was to come. Jesus, going to the cross, the highest example of serving all of humanity, taught his disciples what it meant to be great.

AT THIS MOMENT OF GREATEST CLOSENESS to God, filled with the absolute confidence of knowing where he came from, to whom he belonged, and where he was going, Jesus came even closer to humanity, choosing to perform the role of a servant. Losing nothing, he showed that greatness doesn't consist only of the large things, the heroic deeds, the important missions, but is also built on attention to the human touch that acknowledges "I know you, and you matter to me." Throughout his ministry, we see Jesus touching people, touching the unlovely, healing the sick with a touch. "There is no part of you I do not love," he seems to say, "no wound, no sore, no amount of this world's dirt that I cannot wash away."

> *Lord, let us be like Jesus.*
> *Let us understand that the highest and best*
> *demonstration of his love*
> *is sometimes serving on our knees*
> *where your love and your servants*
> *are most needed.*

Disciples at the Last Supper

John 13:34–35

> "... A new commandment I give to you, that
> you love one another; even as I have loved you,
> that you also love one another. By this all men
> will know that you are my disciples, if you have
> love for one another."

The Passover meal had most likely been celebrated
by every disciple and Jesus every year of their lives.
The disciples had been charged by Jesus to find the
room where the Passover feast was to be held, and
they were told to prepare the meal for the group. The
entire Passover meal was a dramatic, symbolic enact-
ment of the flight of the Jews from their captivity in
Egypt. Each element of the meal was a reminder of
some part of the captivity in Egypt or the nature of
their flight.

After the sacrifice of the lamb at the temple, there
followed the preparation of the meal. There was a
ceremonial search for and destruction of all leaven

in the house, and then the lamb was to be roasted in a certain way, and herbs and bread were to be prepared. The work of the disciples thus changed from accompanying Jesus as he taught in the outward, busy world teeming with people to the more inward, focused domestic acts of chopping up apples for the *charosheth,* cleaning the herbs, and cooking the lamb. Perhaps the disciples joked and talked as they oversaw the preparation of the meal for the others.

The account of the Passover meal in John is more extended than in any of the other Gospels. The public teaching of Jesus had ended, and in John we see him giving his disciples his final words. While our reading of his teaching is always accompanied by our knowledge of the crucifixion and the resurrection, the disciples, despite all of Jesus' statements, still do not seem to understand that Jesus is now giving them parting words, a final statement of his knowledge and wisdom.

WHAT WAS IN THE DISCIPLES' HEARTS and minds during this Passover feast? Much of what we read shows that they were still a very self-centered lot. In the shadow of the cross, according to one Gospel, they dispute over which is the greatest. The Master washes their feet, assuming the role of servant, and none offers to assist. Jesus says that one of them is to betray him, and each is concerned more about whether he is the one rather than seeking to protect Jesus from betrayal. And yet, this was the bunch to whom Jesus was entrusting his ministry, the continuation of the new covenant. Just as the Passover feast dramatized the flight of the Jews from Egypt, so is Jesus teaching his disciples to flee from their old ways of thinking and acting. He exhorts them to follow a new rule, a rule of love. In the future, everyone will know they are disciples of Jesus because of how they loved one another.

As we focus inward during Lent, a time set aside for reflection and contemplation, what is our Egypt that we need to flee? What are we enslaved to today, and what Promised Land are we bound for? Can we hear the urgency in Jesus' voice when he speaks to us through his words to the disciples? How well are we living the new law of love in all that we do?

God of the flight from Egypt,
help us to flee what enslaves us
and follow you to the Promised Land.

On the Way to the Garden of Gethsemane

Luke 22:39

And he came out, and went, as was his custom, to the Mount of Olives; and the disciples followed him.

The pause before the storm. The moment before the doctor says the words that will change our life forever. The peaceful laughing moment before the phone rings. The last day of vacation before we return to the grind. The last time with friends before we all part to go to college and different futures. There is a bittersweetness about the lingering time when the status quo is the most safe — when we feel snug and secure in the warmth of our dreams or wishes fulfilled or our ignorance of what lies ahead. We cling to it, sometimes knowing that in the very next minute life will change and we will desperately wish we were back in that minute before, the time when all was still okay and the next minute and a changed future had not yet arrived. It is hard to go back to the innocence of "before" once we have been changed by the "after." We may seek desperately to return to the time when all was not as it is now, but those efforts may succeed only in part or may succeed only when we anesthetize ourselves enough.

The Last Supper for Jesus and the disciples was the pregnant pause. As they walked in the darkness toward the Mount of Olives, Jesus was still with his friends, his friends who had sworn their bravery and their willingness to stand firm at his side and had not yet been proven false, and Jesus' life and direction were still in his own hands. They were a tired group of men, full from their meal, perhaps calm now that the intensity of the ceremonial preparations was over, solemn from the reminder of deliverance preserved in the hymns sung and the religious rituals completed. Perhaps they were quiet, emotionally drained from the intensity of Jesus' words to them, still puzzling over the content, but sensitive that this was not the time to seek further clarification. The crunch of their footsteps on the dry ground as they moved through the valley of Kidron to the gardens. The gnarled and twisted forms of the olive trees dark against the sky. The receding sounds of the city. The low murmurs and occasional laughter from other groups of people returning from their Passover dinners in Jerusalem to their overnight lodging.

WHEN WE ARE IN THE "AFTER" it is too late to change anything. We will be enmeshed where we are, with the new knowledge, the new event, the new place, and all we have left of the "before" are our memories or the strength we gained or the resources we developed. Sometimes, aware of the change to come, we hesitate, we linger.

Lord, help us to understand
that sometimes we need to pause with you
before we take the next step,
sometimes we need the respite
of a stroll in the valley
before we reach our own Garden of Gethsemane,
sometimes we need to linger
in between hearing and acting upon your word,
we need to tarry just a while longer
to absorb what we have heard from you.
But not too long, not too long . . .
for life and the working out of your will await us,
just as the Garden, Judas, the cross
—and the resurrection—
awaited Jesus.

Jesus Praying in the Garden

Mark 14:32-36

And they went to a place which was called Gethsemane; and he said to his disciples, "Sit here, while I pray." And he took with him Peter and James and John, and began to be greatly distressed and troubled. And he said to them, "My soul is very sorrowful, even to death; remain here and watch." And going a little farther, he fell on the ground and prayed that, if it were possible, the hour might pass from him. And he said, "Abba, Father, all things are possible to thee; remove this cup from me; yet not what I will, but what thou wilt."

The city of Jerusalem at the time of Jesus had no gardens due to the restrictions on the use of the carefully prescribed space for the Holy City. Therefore, a few wealthy people had areas set aside for gardens on the

Mount of Olives, which was reached by leaving Jerusalem, crossing the Kidron Valley, and then ascending once again to the hill that looked across to Jerusalem. It is there that the Garden of Gethsemane lies. It was probably owned by a friend of Jesus who offered him the use of the Garden, and we read in Luke that Jesus was in the custom of going to the Garden. The historian Josephus has estimated that over two million people were in Jerusalem during the Passover, so space apart from the crowds, time undisturbed, would have been both hard to come by and very welcome. Jesus knew he needed this time apart, out in the open, as close to God as he could possibly get, before the end approached.

Jesus' time in the Garden at Gethsemane is the turning point of the Passion week. It is the waiting room between the three years of Jesus' ministry and the death and resurrection that he knows must happen. It is the time when all of Jesus' resolve and fierce determination collide with the human fear of the pain to come. This is the place where Jesus had to choose whether to go forward or to turn aside, with our salvation awaiting the decision. We read the accounts of Jesus praying, in agony, and we find a glimpse of the absolute intimacy and dependence that Jesus felt with God. We cannot even imagine the pain God too must have felt, watching, feeling, knowing what he was asking of Jesus. We see Jesus seeking human comfort and finding none, and we almost turn our head away. We are walking on most sacred ground here, and the tension is palpable. Jesus did not fully understand why his Father was asking him to do this, why this sacrifice was necessary. In this way, Jesus too was like us, he was asked to follow God even when the way and the reasons were not clear.

WE READ WITH HORROR news coming out of war-torn countries, stories of neighbor betraying neighbor, of the ripping apart of families, where children have no childhood except one of violence, hunger, and degradation. There is no choice that is not devastating to someone. Some choices are too dreadful to contemplate. It is terrifying to imagine ourselves in our own Garden of Gethsemane. We too would pray that this cup would pass by us. When we are beset on all sides, when not a single choice we see is a favorable one or maybe even a fair one, when we see no good and right choices, only bad and worse, an emptiness invades the soul, a numbness or a desperation. We know from this account of Jesus praying in the Garden that Jesus knew the depths of human existence. He faced death and pleaded for a different outcome, but in the end he resolved to submit to God's will. He stood up and faced his would-be captors with peace and control.

God, help us to know that at such times,
our place is on our knees,
searching and seeking for your will
and the strength to follow through
what is given for us to do.

Disciples in the Garden

Mark 14:32–35, 37a, 39–43, 50

And they went to a place which was called Gethsemane; and he said to his disciples, "Sit here, while I pray." And he took with him Peter and James and John, and began to be greatly distressed and troubled. And he said to them, "My soul is very sorrowful, even to death; remain here and watch." And going a little farther, he fell on the ground and prayed that, if it were possible, the hour might pass from him. . . . And he came and found them sleeping. . . . And again he went away and prayed, saying the same words. And again he came and found them sleeping, for their eyes were very heavy; and they did not know what to answer him. And he came the third time, and said to them, "Are you still sleeping and taking your rest? It is enough; the hour has come; the Son of man is betrayed into the hands of sinners. Rise, let us be going; see, my betrayer is at hand." And immediately, while he was still speaking, Judas came, one of the twelve, and with him a crowd with swords and clubs, from the chief priests and the scribes and the elders. . . . And they all forsook him and fled.

From the time that Jesus and his disciples began the journey to Jerusalem, Jesus had spoken quite directly of the events that were to happen to him, as well as more apocalyptic matters. Even at the Passover meal, Jesus had said that one of the disciples would betray him and had made cryptic statements regarding the bread and the cup being his body and blood. Following the Passover meal, Jesus and the disciples went back out of Jerusalem to the Garden of Gethsemane on the Mount of Olives. Jesus took Peter, James, and John with him as he went further up to pray; Jesus did not want to face the darkness of this night alone. He asked the disciples to wait and watch while he prayed, but the disciples, tired after long days and demands and hard work, gradually lost the fight and sleep took over. We read that Jesus woke the disciples two times, asking for their comforting presence or warning them of the need to prepare for what was to come, and each time the disciples fell back asleep. The third time they awoke to the presence of the crowd that came to claim Jesus for the cross.

We never imagine that what has been predicted

will actually arrive now, not now when it is inconvenient. Wait until we are rested and have the strength to cope. But for the weary disciples, the dark time did arrive, the crowd did enter the Garden, and the events that led to the cross began their inexorable movement forward. The time for waiting and preparing was over, and the disciples had missed their opportunity.

I T IS IN THE GARDEN where we last see the disciples all together as a group until after the resurrection. We read that they fled the Garden in the face of the arrival of the Judas-led, torch-lit crowd of police and priests. We do not read of all of them being in the crowd when Pilate offers a choice between Jesus and Barabbas. Nor do we read of the disciples as a group being present at the crucifixion. Thus, the time in the Garden is all the more poignant for it is the last opportunity Jesus had to see the faces of the men he had labored with and taught, exhorted, and befriended over the past three years. But they were not emotionally with him, offering reassurance or support; instead, a powerful tiredness overwhelmed them and they slept. What regret must have filled them in the days that followed!

We don't always recognize turning points when they come. No neon signs, no crescendo of background music alerting us to "Pay Attention! This

Is an Important Moment!" The thoughts of parents or relatives of one who has died suddenly, tragically, are anguished, regret-filled: if only I had said, "I love you," when he went off to work; if only I had read one more bedtime story; if only I had expressed my love when she was here to hear it; if only I hadn't nursed my anger, been so rigid, been such a stickler for routine. We want reassurance that our beloved ones entered the eternal surrounded by the deep knowledge that they were loved and loved dearly.

Lord, help us to show our love,
to give the gift of ourselves, our best,
our loving support now, at every opportunity.
Let us tell others we care
and learn to demonstrate our care.
If we are to have regrets,
let them not be about
how we treated those we loved
in the days of our lives.

Malchus

Luke 22:47-51

While he was still speaking, there came a crowd, and the man called Judas, one of the twelve, was leading them. He drew near to Jesus to kiss him; but Jesus said to him, "Judas, would you betray the Son of man with a kiss?" And when those who were about him saw what would follow, they said, "Lord, shall we strike with the sword?" And one of them struck the slave of the high priest and cut off his right ear. But Jesus said, "No more of this!" And he touched his ear and healed him.

John 18:10

Then Simon Peter, having a sword, drew it and struck the high priest's slave and cut off his right ear. The slave's name was Malchus.

Did anyone entering the Garden of Gethsemane that night to arrest Jesus want anyone hurt? Jesus was there to pray and took his disciples with him for comfort and company. Judas led the religious authorities and soldiers to Jesus, anticipating that a kiss would be the only physical effort of the night. Perhaps the soldiers anticipated that some force might be needed, and so they were ready for anything. The religious authorities perhaps acknowledged force as a regrettable but necessary part of the operation. A servant of the high priest was probably along just to carry the torch or to see to his master's wishes. Surrounded by so many soldiers and so many religious leaders, even in the dark, the servant would not have felt threatened.

And yet, this servant was the only one we read of who was physically hurt in the events in the Garden. Simon Peter raised a sword in an attempt to protect Jesus from capture and cut off the ear of this servant, a servant the Gospel of John tells us was named Malchus. Jesus healed the ear and rebuked Peter, saying, "No more of this!" It is unlikely that Malchus would ever forget such an incident. He had come to assist in the taking of this man, but of all that he expected to happen that night, he most likely did not expect that he would be the object of healing by the very rabbi they had come to arrest. How was it that John knew the name of this servant? Perhaps we know his name because Jesus healed more than his ear that night, because something of the eternal was given to Malchus as well. Perhaps he also came to follow Jesus.

A MAN GETS HIS EAR CUT OFF by a brave disciple ready to take on the world — a statistic. Malchus, a servant, loses an ear to a brave defender of the rabbi Jesus and has his own wound healed by the one who is arrested — a story. The difference between a statistic and a story is the presence of a name. A name conveys a specific person, someone who has a history, a family, a reality. We can live with statistics, which provide a safe buffer for our emotions between people and a problem to be solved. We find it harder to manage our emotions about Vanessa, who was abused, John, who was robbed, or Mrs. Garcia who was killed by a drunk driver named Jamie. We can feel so nameless, despite the frequent use of our name in all the false and canned friendliness of salespeople determined to be our new best friend. We find our individual stories subsumed in statistics in the paper: "Oh, I was one of a hundred thousand people diagnosed with cancer in the Midwest this year." I'm not unique, I'm not special, I don't matter. The leaps in our minds are not difficult ones to make. Yet, Jesus always sees us as individuals. There are no statistics in God's kingdom, only people who have been called by name, created by name, died for by name.

> *Thank you, God,*
> *for knowing and caring about me,*
> *a child you have called by name.*

Judas

John 12:3-6

Mary took a pound of costly ointment of pure nard and anointed the feet of Jesus and wiped his feet with her hair; and the house was filled with the fragrance of the ointment. But Judas Iscariot, one of his disciples (he who was to betray him), said, "Why was this ointment not sold for three hundred denarii and given to the poor?" This he said, not that he cared for the poor but because he was a thief, and as he had the money box he used to take what was put into it.

Luke 22:3-6

Then Satan entered into Judas called Iscariot, who was of the number of the twelve; he went away and conferred with the chief priests and officers how he might betray him to them. And they were glad, and engaged to give him money.

So he agreed, and sought an opportunity to betray him to them in the absence of the multitude.

Matthew 27:1–7

When morning came, all the chief priests and the elders of the people took counsel against Jesus to put him to death; and they bound him and led him away and delivered him to Pilate the governor.

When Judas, his betrayer, saw that he was condemned, he repented and brought back the thirty pieces of silver to the chief priests and the elders, saying, "I have sinned in betraying innocent blood." They said, "What is that to us? See to it yourself." And throwing down the pieces of silver in the temple, he departed; and he went and hanged himself. But the chief priests, taking the pieces of silver, said, "It is not lawful to put them into the treasury, since they are blood money." So they took counsel, and bought with them the potter's field, to bury strangers in.

The images of Judas from one view seem so clear: he was the disciple who had stolen money from the communal purse, who had raised false concerns about giving money to the poor when Mary anointed Jesus' feet with the precious ointment, and who was a zealot, one who was committed to overthrowing the yoke of the Roman government by any means necessary, including violent ones. He was the one who sought out the chief priests and promised to lead them to Jesus, willing to betray even the closest friend for personal gain. And when he saw the events unleashed by his betrayal of Jesus, according to Matthew, he committed suicide. What then can we learn from the story of Judas?

W E STRUGGLE WITH JUDAS. Knowing that Judas would betray him, nonetheless, Jesus chose him to be one of the twelve, the only non-Galilean. Why? And what motivated Judas to betray Jesus? The monetary amount was slight, and yet Judas bargained over it. Some have conjectured he wanted to force Jesus' hand, to force him to become the kind of Messiah Judas and other nationalists dreamed about. If so, Judas was guilty of betraying Jesus for not being who Judas wanted him to be, for failing to live up to Judas's expectations. And yet, God's plans used the death of Jesus to lead to the resurrection, and Judas was one instrument who led to the death of Jesus. We too wonder in a breath-holding, agonizing way if we have it in us to be Judas.

Perhaps the most painful part of Judas's story is

told in Matthew, when he returned to the chief priests after the judgment and condemnation of Jesus. We picture Judas, eyes wild, hair disheveled, rushing in to see the priests, those who had been so eager and friendly before. His hands are trembling and clutching at the bag with the thirty coins, the price of betrayal. Now aloof, disdainful, the chief priests pull back in distaste, as Judas insistently, urgently, begs and pleads to give back the money in a pitiful attempt to exchange the coins for Jesus, as if the money were really what was at stake. Horror filling his face, the blood ringing in his ears, the madness entering his mind as he realizes the full extent of what he has done, Judas rushes out, scattering coins all over the floor, looking in agony for a way out, any way out, of the terror filling his soul. And finally, death at his own hand.

If we use the text from Matthew, then we are to feel tremendous pity for Judas, for he was then the only one among all the priests and Roman leaders and others who participated in the actions that led to the condemnation and execution of Christ who actually realized the full extent of who was being put to death — the Son of God.

> *Lord, we can set in motion,*
> *even without knowing,*
> *ever-widening ripples of events.*

Help us to align
all that we are
and all that we do with your will.
Help us to know as well
that even at the end of the terror-filled rush
away from what we have done,
that you still stand there,
ready to forgive,
ready to accept our repentance,
ready to open the gates of Paradise —
even when it is you we have betrayed.

The High Priest's
Maid

Mark 14:66–70

*And as Peter was below in the courtyard, one
of the maids of the high priest came; and seeing
Peter warming himself, she looked at him, and
said, "You also were with the Nazarene, Jesus."
But he denied it, saying, "I neither know nor
understand what you mean." And he went out
into the gateway. And the maid saw him, and
began again to say to the bystanders, "This man
is one of them." But again he denied it. And
after a little while again the bystanders said to
Peter, "Certainly you are one of them; for you
are a Galilean."*

In the Academy Award–winning film *The Remains
of the Day* and in the novel by Kazuo Ishiguro
from which the film was taken, the central figure
of the story is a man who served as the butler in a

large, aristocratic English household. Because of his position, he had seen and met many of the major political figures of the day. He knew and was required to remember their preferences — sleeping with the windows open or closed, pants pressed with a crease or without, favorite menu selections and beverage preferences. Later, when the butler goes on vacation, he tries to impress a few village residents with all the people of prominence whom he has known, assuming the persona of a participant in international affairs. However, the butler knew little and thought less about the political issues of the day and can say nothing of, or provide any insight about, the actions of these men on the world stage, only of the daily pressures of catering to their needs.

The world of small details and the world of greater vision so often exist side by side, intertwined. Likewise, in poignant and sharp counterpoint to the high drama between the powerful Sanhedrin and Jesus occurring inside the high priest's house, Matthew tells a story of another drama, this time placed outside the imposing chamber, among the servants of the high priest as they sat around the fire in the courtyard. Waiting until they would be called upon to perform some task or to fetch someone or something that was needed, perhaps they engaged in idle speculation about the prisoner — his Galilean accent, his linen tunic. Here, around this fire, Peter appears. In a direct echo of the questioning of Jesus in front of his accusers, the high priest's maid asks Peter several times if he was a follower of the man who is currently undergoing questioning by the Sanhedrin.[7] "Weren't you with him? I can tell by your accent that you come from the same place." We are unsure why she keeps coming back to this, trying to tie Peter to the Nazarene rabbi. We might think it is so that she can find out more about Jesus, learn more of this man who has caused such an uproar. But from the way in which the story is told, it would seem that perhaps she, like the butler, can pay attention only to the outer significance and details of the thing rather than to the deeper substance.

HOW TENACIOUS AND PERSISTENT are we in matters that in the long run really don't count? Why do we get so worked up over these insignificant matters? Is it because we can grasp them and so much of the rest of our lives seems beyond us or out of our control? Is it because we are willing to express emotion and tangle with others over a fact or an inconsequential point rather than to confront that which is causing deeper conflict in our relationship? Or have we really become so shallow and petty that we really do care more about the butler's details than about the larger issues?

God, grant us the gift of discernment
to recognize what you care about.
Help us to recalibrate
our measures of importance
so that we may gauge the value
of what really matters
in life and in serving you.

Peter

Mark 14:53–54, 66–72

And they led Jesus to the high priest; and all the chief priests and the elders and the scribes were assembled. And Peter had followed him at a distance, right into the courtyard of the high priest; and he was sitting with the guards, and warming himself at the fire. . . .

And as Peter was below in the courtyard, one of the maids of the high priest came; and seeing Peter warming himself, she looked at him, and said, "You also were with the Nazarene, Jesus." But he denied it, saying, "I neither know nor understand what you mean." And he went out into the gateway. And the maid saw him, and began again to say to the bystanders, "This man is one of them." But again he denied it. And after a little while again the bystanders said to Peter, "Certainly you are one of them; for you are a Galilean." But he began to invoke a curse on himself and to swear, "I do not know this man of whom you speak." And immediately the cock crowed a second time. And Peter remembered how Jesus had said to him, "Before the cock crows twice, you will deny me three times." And he broke down and wept.

Peter is present at so many of the key events of Jesus' ministry. By turns impetuous, rash, fervent, passionate, Peter was the first to recognize Jesus' divinity. He was one of Jesus' inner circle, chosen by Jesus to be with him in his darkest time, as he prayed in the Garden of Gethsemane. Although Peter and the other unnamed disciple (probably John) were the only ones identified as having the courage to follow Jesus into the very center of danger, what we remember is Peter denying that he knew Jesus three times, an event Jesus had foretold. Those sitting around the fire where Peter warmed himself were servants of the high priest, so it would not be unreasonable for Peter to assume that revealing his relationship to Jesus to them could prove hazardous, especially since we learn that one of the questioners was a relative of the servant whose ear he had slashed off. Truth can be a dangerous thing. The alarm call of truth, the cock crowing, woke Peter from his fog of fear and anxiety, and he instantly realized what he had done. For one so confident, so sure in his love for Jesus, his actions were a bitter disappointment, more so to

Peter than to anyone. Yet, the story of his denials must have come from Peter himself.

Denial of Jesus, denial of the truth. Denial is such a standard gambit these days by those confronted with an unpleasant truth about their actions that we seldom believe it. "I knew nothing about it," says the public figure. "I didn't see anything" says the potential witness. "I never met the person before," says the celebrity. Often, the denial is itself later denied by saying they were quoted out of context or the complete statement wasn't available.

Why do we deny the truth? We deny because we can't accept our own actions, because we want to delay the ramifications of our actions, because we don't want to lose what we have, because we hope it will all blow over or the public will lose interest. We deny because when we did the difficult thing, we had lost the ability to see what was wrong about what we did. The times, the compromises, the actions of those around us made that little action of ours seem so small in comparison. Or what we did was a "reward" for all the hard choices we navigated so successfully. We deny we have a drinking problem or a substance abuse problem or even that we were wrong. When we deny something, it extends the fiction, the fairy tale just a little longer. Our lives are as perfect, as problem free as we pretend, if we just deny the truth a little longer.

When do we deny Jesus? When we know the right thing, the thing that Jesus would want us to do, and we don't do it, we deny Jesus. When we don't stand up for our faith, we deny Jesus. When we turn our back on a need we feel compelled to meet, we deny Jesus. We prize truth, we say "don't tell lies" to our children, and yet the one to whom we lie the most is ourselves. We deny we hear the Spirit leading us; we deny the truth we know about ourselves.

> *Help us, Lord,*
> *oh, help us to face ourselves,*
> *our lives,*
> *our choices squarely,*
> *to speak out and live out*
> *our relationship to you.*

Annas

John 18:12–14, 19–24

So the band of soldiers and their captain and the officers of the Jews seized Jesus and bound him. First they led him to Annas; for he was the father-in-law of Caiaphas, who was high priest that year. It was Caiaphas who had given counsel to the Jews that it was expedient that one man should die for the people.... The high priest then questioned Jesus about his disciples and his teaching. Jesus answered him, "I have spoken openly to the world; I have always taught in synagogues and in the temple, where all Jews come together; I have said nothing secretly. Why do you ask me? Ask those who have heard me, what I said to them; they know what I said." When he had said this, one of the officers standing by struck Jesus with his hand, saying, "Is that how you answer the high priest?" Jesus answered him, "If I have spoken wrongly, bear witness to the wrong; but if I have

spoken rightly, why do you strike me?" An-
nas then sent him bound to Caiaphas the high
priest.

We read only in John that Jesus was first brought before Annas, the father-in-law of Caiaphas, the high
priest. Annas had himself been high priest for a de-
cade, and four of his sons had held the same position.
The role of high priest, under Roman rule, was filled
by one who was willing to collaborate with the Romans. Annas was quite rich, and bribery was used to
propel him and his sons into office. It is said that the
markets inside the temple precincts (where acceptable animal sacrifices could be purchased at vastly
inflated rates) were called the Bazaars of Annas and
were owned by the family of Annas. The family was
quite notorious and is even mentioned in the Jewish
Talmud as "serpents." Thus, Jesus had attacked the
vested interests of Annas when he had swept through
the temple markets. Annas wanted to ensure the absence of this Galilean troublemaker in the manner
of those who have sought to protect ill-gotten gains
throughout the centuries: he wanted Jesus killed.[8]

A NNAS IS A FIGURE OF CORRUPTION of the worst
kind. In the guise and position of great faith and
piety, bearing responsibility for working alternately
with or against the Romans to maintain the freedom

of Jews to worship in this Roman-ruled province, he used his position for personal gain and profit, for power and status. Annas served as the power behind the throne, guiding the positions and practices of his sons and son-in-law during their terms as high priest, making sure the family's wealth was protected while at the same time enjoying the ability to play high-stakes political chess games with the Romans. Annas's son-in-law Caiaphas says in John 11:47–50, following the raising of Lazarus from the dead, that it is "expedient" for one man to die that the whole nation should not perish, and therefore Jesus should be killed. Caiaphas is speaking on behalf of the existing power structure and his family's political and financial interests, which they held in uneasy collaboration with the Romans. All of this power flowed from and through Annas.

We act like Annas when we speak, act, vote, or take positions with self-righteous care for the interests of the community, but when in fact we are primarily driven by a self-interest that seeks to exclude not include, protect not share, and elevate our station while oppressing the standards of others. We act like Annas when we abuse positions of responsibility, whether or not for financial gain, when we make decisions that deny the value of every individual, when we continue to choose the path of conflict instead of looking for the way that heals and uplifts.

We, too, act like Annas when we use the language and the image and the power of religion to achieve personal benefit.

> God, help us to know our motives
> when we speak in your language.
> Help us to discern
> when self-interest is getting in the way
> or subverting the greater interest
> of our communities.
> Help us to be accountable to you
> for the actions we take in your name.

Caiaphas

Matthew 26:57, 59–60a, 62–64a, 65–66

*Then those who had seized Jesus led him to
Caiaphas the high priest, where the scribes and
the elders had gathered.... Now the chief priests
and the whole council sought false testimony
against Jesus that they might put him to death,
but they found none, although many false witnesses came forward.... And the high priest
stood up and said, "Have you no answer to
make? What is it that these men testify against
you?" But Jesus was silent. And the high priest
said to him, "I adjure you by the living God,
tell us if you are the Christ, the Son of God?"
Jesus said to him, "You have said so...." Then
the high priest tore his robes, and said, "He
has uttered blasphemy. Why do we still need
witnesses? You have now heard his blasphemy.
What is your judgment?" They answered, "He
deserves death."*

As the high priest, Caiaphas was the head of the Jewish Sanhedrin, which was like a Supreme Court. He was the religious head of the Jewish people and represented the people in front of the Roman authorities. Alone in the entire Roman empire, the Jews enjoyed some measure of religious freedom. It was Caiaphas's job to ensure that this relative ability to exercise their faith was preserved. Thus, part religious head, part appeaser of the Romans, Caiaphas was also responsible for ensuring that the Jews themselves did nothing to disturb the uneasy truce.

Caiaphas had the right under Roman law to appeal to the emperor in complaint against the procurator, or governor, of Palestine. On at least three prior occasions, Pontius Pilate and Caiaphas had gone head to head and Caiaphas had won. It was a longstanding, bitter, high-stakes battle of politics, and Caiaphas wanted to make sure that he kept the upper hand. He did not want to upset the delicate balance with Rome that permitted the Jews to keep their temple and their religious traditions alive. Caiaphas had the right to have his own police force; however, he did not have the authority to put anyone to death, a right reserved strictly for the Romans. While Caiaphas's quarrel with Jesus had many levels, only a certain kind of charge against Jesus would matter enough to the Romans to justify the death penalty. Caiaphas could not bring Jesus to Pontius

Pilate on a religious charge of blasphemy, which Pilate would dismiss out of hand. Instead, Caiaphas had to have a charge that was political in nature, one that a Roman would find adequate to condemn a man. While Caiaphas knew that Pilate would see through the political charges he stated against Jesus, he also knew that one more blunder by Pilate, one more appeal by Caiaphas to the emperor, and Pilate was finished. Caiaphas held the upper hand, even if Pilate had the authority.

How do we find a way to relate to Caiaphas? What in the consummate political chess player speaks to us? Caiaphas says that it was expedient for one man to die that all of Jerusalem should not perish. Most of our decisions do not reach the level of determining the religious fate of thousands of people. Perhaps, then, what we see in Caiaphas is the ultimate example of what happens when we get further and further away from the simple basics of our faith, when we become immersed in games and compromises and scorekeeping in the places we live and work, until God is gradually only a footnote to the real game afoot. We become enamored with our own cleverness, our own skills. Caiaphas was a very clever player, knowing how to inflame and how to cool, willing to break all the rules and yet feign indignation when others acted likewise, having the ability to conjure up moral outrage yet able to assess a new religious teacher only as friend or foe. When our compass has as its true north the maintenance of our position at the expense of morality, then we are like Caiaphas.

> God, *we would ask that we be given*
> *the gift of a direct faith,*
> *a faith that points to you without hesitation.*

The Sanhedrin

Matthew 26:59–60a, 65–68, 27:1–2

Now the chief priests and the whole council sought false testimony against Jesus that they might put him to death, but they found none, though many false witnesses came forward.... Then the high priest tore his robes and said, "He has uttered blasphemy. Why do we still need witnesses? You have now heard his blasphemy. What is your judgment?" They answered, "He deserves death." Then they spat in his face and struck him; and some slapped him, saying, "Prophesy to us, you Christ! Who is it that struck you?"...

When morning came, all the chief priests and the elders of the people took counsel against Jesus to put him to death; and they bound him and led him away and delivered him to Pilate the governor.

They gathered with a sense of bustling importance, called away from Passover celebrations out into the night for a trial of a radical, difficult, enigmatic, challenging rabbi. Hurried through a courtyard lit by torches into the high priest's house, the religious authorities gathered into self-important groups, comparing notes and stories, highly charged gossip. Into the midst of this august assemblage came Jesus, his plain linen tunic still dusty from kneeling to pray in the Garden, his manner exuding quiet confidence, his assured way needing no sycophants or bustling assistants to convey his own unique power. The Sanhedrin fell silent. Some members bristled with the energy that came from knowing this time they held the winning hand, after having been shamed and outwitted by this Jesus, their complexity beaten by his simplicity, their love of endless debate pulled up short by his authoritative answers. They looked forward to seeing Jesus submit to their order. Others were less sure, having recognized the clear insight Jesus had.

There were seventy-one altogether in the Sanhedrin, which was the Jewish Supreme Court, although it is not clear how many of them were actually there that night. Although Luke's account is slightly different, this meeting was being conducted contrary to all their own rules: the trial was being held at night, and all criminal trials were to be held only during the day; it was at the high priest's house instead of in the temple precincts; testimony of Jesus' innocence was not allowed as was required. The list of violations and exceptions to their own rules is long. Yet, their hatred of Jesus was such that even at the end they lost all dignity and fell into physical abuse.

W̲HAT WAS JESUS' CRIME to the Sanhedrin, really? We read that Caiaphas and the Sanhedrin sought false witnesses, but couldn't find anything satisfactory. Obviously, they had a predetermined verdict in mind that required only a few facts, any facts, in support. What was it about Jesus that really galled the members of the Sanhedrin? Was it his attacks and pithy comparisons for them? Did epithets like "whited sepulchers" and "vipers' brood" really hit too hard? Surely for a group accustomed to playing cat-and-mouse games with Pilate, those kinds of words would bounce off their thick skins. Was it that he failed to preserve their mystery, the authority that accompanied their position? In contrast to their sophistry, he spoke in ways the people understood, he made God approachable and real, he gave them stories with characters and situations they could understand. He was one of the people.

What did Jesus so threaten in the Sanhedrin that they were willing to kill Jesus to keep that part safe? What is it in our lives that feels threatened by Jesus? What secret, unidentified little plot of sin or fear or prejudice or need do we want to protect at all costs?

What secrets, what lies do we refuse to admit even to ourselves and cannot bear to expose to Jesus?

Help us, Lord, to let Jesus in,
to allow his healing touch
to melt the fear that is blocking his entry
into all parts of our lives.

False Witnesses at Jesus' Trial

Matthew 26:59–63a

> Now the chief priests and the whole council
> sought false testimony against Jesus that they
> might put him to death, but they found none,
> though many false witnesses came forward. At
> last two came forward and said, "This fellow
> said, 'I am able to destroy the temple of God,
> and to build it in three days.'" And the high
> priest stood up and said, "Have you no an-
> swer to make? What is it that these men testify
> against you?" But Jesus was silent.

According to the rules of the Sanhedrin, to bear false
witness in a capital case, one in which there was
the possibility of passing a death sentence, made the
one who lied liable to be put to death. However, in
the trial of Jesus in front of the Sanhedrin, Matthew
states that the chief priests and the whole council sought false witness against Jesus. Because the
false testimony was actually looked for and searched

out, not just allowed, there may have been some incentives offered to those willing to provide false testimony. Some of the false testimony may have been misstatements of what Jesus said or misrepresentations about what Jesus did. Because so much of what Jesus did was part of a very public ministry, there certainly would have been many who would have heard him speak. Yet, none of the witnesses could agree.

Those who bore false witness in this trial are in the end minor players, ineffective witnesses against Jesus. Caiaphas the high priest had to force Jesus into making the very statement on which Caiaphas would hang his charge of blasphemy. It is that aspect that perhaps speaks to us the most. Jesus had a very compelling ministry, a very public ministry in his last few days in Jerusalem: a dramatic entrance into the city, a cleansing of the temple courts, and angry denunciations of the moneychangers, the sellers of sacrificial animals, and the scribes and Pharisees. He healed people and spoke out publicly, disputed, contended, instructed, and answered the trickiest religious questions that the chief priests and scribes could devise. And yet, the best these poor witnesses had to offer were inconsequential, ineffective mumblings and rantings.

What kind of witness are we for Jesus? Would we know enough of Jesus, exude enough evidence of the power he has in our lives, that our testimony would clearly and convincingly identify Jesus as the Son of God? How strong a witness is our life? Do people see Jesus in our life, or are we a weak and ineffective statement about him? Shouldn't our lives, the way we live, the choices we make, the manner in which we treat others, show to whom we belong?

> Help us, God, to be effective witnesses
> of your power to change lives
> and to act in the world today.
> Help us to live lives
> that provide compelling evidence
> that Jesus is alive!

Pontius Pilate

Matthew 27:1-2, 11-20, 24, 26

When morning came, all the chief priests and the elders of the people took counsel against Jesus to put him to death; and they bound him and led him away and delivered him to Pilate the governor....

Now Jesus stood before the governor; and the governor asked him, "Are you the King of the Jews?" Jesus said to him, "You have said so." But when he was accused by the chief priests and elders, he made no answer. Then Pilate said to him, "Do you not hear how many things they testify against you?" But he gave him no answer, not even to a single charge; so that the governor wondered greatly.

Now at the feast the governor was accustomed to release for the crowd any one prisoner whom they wanted. And they had then a notorious prisoner, called Barabbas. So when they had gathered, Pilate said to them, "Whom do you want me to release for you, Barabbas or Jesus who is called Christ?" For he knew that it was out of envy that they had delivered him up. Besides, while he was sitting on the judgment seat, his wife sent word to him, "Have nothing to do with that righteous man, for I have suffered much over him today in a dream." Now the chief priests and the elders persuaded the people to ask for Barabbas and destroy Jesus....

So when Pilate saw that he was gaining nothing, but rather that a riot was beginning, he took water and washed his hands before the crowd, saying, "I am innocent of this man's blood; see to it yourselves."... Then he released for them Barabbas, and having scourged Jesus, delivered him to be crucified.

Pontius Pilate was clearly not the rising star of the Roman political world, for he was stuck in the back of nowhere, in a post that was neither safe nor particularly prestigious. He was putting in time, enjoying all the spoils of being a petty potentate, with the heavy hand of power in his little corner of the empire. His normal place of residency was Caesarea, but at times when there was a likelihood of unrest, usually feast times, he was expected to be present in Jerusalem. His track record with the Jews was not great: he had been in several serious squabbles with Caiaphas, where Pilate's bull-headedness and unwillingness to bow to local religious customs had come up short against the Jewish insistence upon observing its own laws, a concession no other Roman governor in the empire had to make. Yet, the Jewish leaders relied on the Romans to do for them what their own rules did not allow, and in return the Jewish authorities kept the populace under control and prevented the kind of uprising that had happened in so many other outposts of the empire. It was a system of uneasy accommodation.

But occasionally, even one accustomed to compromise will look at what is being asked and chafe under the restrictions. In front of him was an itinerant preacher who apparently claimed to be the king of the Jews. He had no army, he bore no weapons, his followers were nonviolent. Pilate by now had certainly learned what a revolutionary looked like, and Jesus wasn't it. Yet, the religious authorities felt threatened. They wanted this Jesus gone. Pilate tried to find a way that even his speckled and gray conscience could approve of, and the effort fell short. Finally, unable to say no, but unwilling to say yes, he turned it over to the people to let them decide. Then in a symbolic act, he washed his hands of responsibility for the decision of the crowd.

AS WE ASSUME MORE RESPONSIBILITIES, we may find that the pressure to compromise becomes more urgent. As we know more of life, we see so much gray and less black and white. We find reasons for not acting, for not speaking, for not participating. Then something happens or we encounter someone who has not lived a life of compromise, and we see in stark contrast the ideals we once held so fiercely, the dreams we once had for our future — and where we are today. Somewhere along the way, we gave away control of our actions, we gave "financial security" or "job security" or "community reputation" control. Sometimes we gave away pieces of ourselves with love, as with our children or spouse. Other times we gave away pieces out of fear or insecurity. Gradually, we were bound in hundreds of tiny, but fiercely strong, strings, all held by someone or something else, unable to act. And so we become Pilate. Is this the cost of fear, the price we pay for clinging to our insecurity? Conversely, do we demand control of others as a price of love?

> *God, give us the courage*
> *to keep our consciences free enough*
> *to act in accordance with your will,*
> *and help us allow others*
> *the same freedom as well.*

Herod

Mark 6:14, 16–20

King Herod heard of it; for Jesus' name had become known.... But when Herod heard of it he said, "John, whom I beheaded, has been raised." For Herod had sent and seized John, and bound him in prison for the sake of Herodias, his brother Philip's wife; because he had married her. For John said to Herod, "It is not lawful for you to have your brother's wife." And Herodias had a grudge against him, and wanted to kill him. But she could not, for Herod feared John, knowing that he was a righteous and holy man, and kept him safe. When he heard him, he was much perplexed; and yet he heard him gladly.

Luke 23:4–12

And Pilate said to the chief priests and the multitudes, "I find no crime in this man." But they were urgent, saying, "He stirs up the people, teaching throughout all Judea, from Galilee even to this place."

When Pilate heard this, he asked whether the man was a Galilean. And when he learned that he belonged to Herod's jurisdiction, he sent him over to Herod, who was himself in Jerusalem at that time. When Herod saw Jesus, he was very glad, for he had long desired to see him, because he had heard about him, and he was hoping to see some sign by him. So he questioned him at some length; but he made no answer. The chief priests and the scribes stood by vehemently accusing him. And Herod with his soldiers treated him with contempt and mocked him; then, arraying him in gorgeous apparel, he sent him back to Pilate. And Herod and Pilate became friends with each other that very day, for before this they had been at enmity with each other.

In one of Pontius Pilate's four attempts to avoid sentencing Jesus to death, he turned Jesus over to Herod Antipas, who was in Jerusalem at the time, because Jesus was from Galilee and Herod was the tetrarch of Galilee. Luke says that Herod was quite pleased to see this Jesus whom he had heard about and wished to see "some sign" by him, as if Jesus were some new magician with a particularly unique set of tricks. Faced with Jesus' silence, Herod and his soldiers began a mockery of their own, which included dressing Jesus in sumptuous robes. Then Herod sent Jesus back to Pilate. Ironically, Luke notes that this episode caused former enemies Herod and Pilate to become friends. The new friendship between Herod and Pilate almost seems to be like a shared wink between two powerful men when faced with a naive youngster with delusions of grandeur.

This account in Luke, however, is not the first appearance of Herod Antipas in the New Testament. Herod Antipas was one of the sons of Herod the Great, who was himself the ruler when Jesus was born, the builder of the temple in Jerusalem, and the one who ordered the slaughter of the babies in Bethlehem at the time of Jesus' birth. In Mark, we read that Herod was apparently fascinated by John the Baptist, alternating between disliking what John said and wanting to listen to more. Herod Antipas had John the Baptist beheaded following an ill-advised promise to his new wife's daughter. In fact, Mark states that when Herod first heard of Jesus he thought Jesus might be John the Baptist come back to life. Thus, in the end, Herod accomplished through indifference what his father sought through violence: the death of Jesus.

WHAT ARE WE TO MAKE of the difference between the Herod who protected and listened to John the Baptist and the Herod who wanted to see Jesus perform a sign and who engaged in crude horseplay? It had cost Herod dearly to see the head of John brought up during a drunken feast, to act as if this horror was a part of an evening's entertainment, this beheading of a prophet, one whom he had admired and listened to. How much easier it was, then, to treat all these men of God as performers, as amusements — raising people from the dead, healing the lame and the blind. Great, show me more! His guilt caused him to slam shut the door to God.

Herod is what happens when we cannot forgive ourselves, when we cannot get over our own past mistakes and believe God could not either. Herod is what happens when we get emotional calluses so thick that no one can ever reach us again. Herod is what we become when we reject the finer reaches of the heart, when out of embarrassment or fear we mock those who have faith, when we fail to understand the ability to believe. Herod is who we become when we are old and tired and cynical and jaded. We take God's great gifts and hurl them in ignorance from our lives.

Help us, God,
to remain open to your possibilities,
to your tenderness,
to your forgiveness.

Crowds before Pontius Pilate

John 18:28

*Then they led Jesus from the house of Caiaphas
to the praetorium. It was early. They themselves
did not enter the praetorium, so that they might
not be defiled, but might eat the passover.*

John 19:1–2, 5–6a, 12–13a, 14b–16

*Then Pilate took Jesus and scourged him. And
the soldiers plaited a crown of thorns and put it
on his head, and arrayed him in a purple robe.
. . . So Jesus came out, wearing the crown of
thorns and the purple robe. Pilate said to them,
"Behold the man!" When the chief priests and
the officers saw him, they cried out, "Crucify
him, crucify him!" . . .*

*Upon this Pilate sought to release him,
but the Jews cried out, "If you release this
man, you are not Caesar's friend; every one*

who makes himself a king sets himself against Caesar." When Pilate heard these words, he brought Jesus out and sat down on the judgment seat. . . . He said to the Jews, "Behold your King!" They cried out, "Away with him, away with him, crucify him!" Pilate said to them, "Shall I crucify your King?" The chief priests answered, "We have no king but Caesar." Then he handed him over to them to be crucified.

We visit the crowds again, this time in front of Pontius Pilate as he turns the decision of which prisoner to release, Jesus or Barabbas, over to the crowds. We are sometimes perplexed by how fickle the crowds of Jerusalem seem to be, one day welcoming Jesus into Jerusalem with waving palm branches, throwing down their cloaks on the road, and then the next, screaming for his crucifixion. The answer is that these are not the same crowds. This was a carefully constructed crowd, of those under obligation to the chief priests, who had been ordered to shout for the release of Barabbas, or of those who were friends of Barabbas. This was the better organized, well-financed crowd of the Sanhedrin and the religious authorities, who, having failed to get their way by lobbying Pontius Pilate, sought to produce a "will of the people." Perhaps the crowds who followed Jesus, those who had been healed or helped, those who had already been rejected by society, the disaffected and the lost, lacked the sophistication, the organization, to recognize what was happening. Events after all had been moving very quickly, and it was really only the members of the Sanhedrin who were on top of the situation. It was this sort of crowd that called for the release of Barabbas and the crucifixion of Jesus.

It is an amazing sequence of events, this strange dance of Pilate and Jesus and the Jewish authorities. The chief priests refuse to defile themselves by coming into Pilate's palace to discuss putting someone to death. The Jewish authorities say that their law demands death — but can't Rome handle the actual crucifixion for them? The cry of the crowd becomes increasingly frenzied, almost hysterical, whipped up and frantic for their howling demands to be granted. "Crucify him, crucify him!" they chanted.

WE ARE REPULSED BY THIS CROWD. We are disgusted by a religious fastidiousness that preserves a ritual cleanliness but feels free to demand the killing of an innocent, but inconvenient, man. We abhor the choice of a murderer over our Jesus. So how do we find something to touch us in this story? Let's look at what the crowd was asking: they wanted their own parochial, personal concerns met, regardless of the cost to others, regardless of the consequences. Think of the sports superstar who creates a demand for a particular kind of athletic shoe and is paid millions to promote it, but the high-priced running shoe is manufactured for pennies by grossly underpaid workers and children who are deemed "lucky to have a job" — and the profits go toward advertising and the millionaire sports star's fee. Buying those shoes perpetuates that economic cycle, but we want, must have, our designer running shoes to go tone and polish our healthy bodies.

When we petulantly want what we want, demand it loudly, insist upon our right to have it, and care little about the consequences of feeding our demand, then we are the crowd in front of Pilate.

> *Lord, help us to recognize in our own lives*
> *the ritual outward cleanliness*
> *that covers up a selfish insistence*
> *for satisfaction at the cost of others.*

Barabbas

Matthew 27:15–17, 20–21, 24, 26

Now at the feast the governor was accustomed to release for the crowd any one prisoner whom they wanted. And they had then a notorious prisoner, called Barabbas. So when they had gathered, Pilate said to them, "Whom do you want me to release for you, Barabbas or Jesus who is called Christ?" ... Now the chief priests and the elders persuaded the people to ask for Barabbas and destroy Jesus. The governor again said to them, "Which of the two do you want me to release for you?" And they said, "Barabbas." ...

So when Pilate saw that he was gaining nothing, but rather that a riot was beginning, he took water and washed his hands before the crowd, saying, "I am innocent of this righteous man's blood; see to it yourselves." ... Then he released for them Barabbas, and having scourged Jesus, delivered him to be crucified.

Barabbas has often been portrayed as a popular charismatic fellow, beside whom Jesus appeared as a defeated ascetic. The Latin phrase of Pilate "Ecce Homo!" or "Behold the man," is seen by some as a mocking statement meant to contrast the pitiable fellow Jesus standing there with the image of a real man. The contrast with Barabbas was intended by the Jewish authorities to put Jesus in a bad light, to make it almost unthinkable to pick Jesus over Barabbas. But Barabbas was a killer, a murderer, not just a likable fellow who was guilty of some minor transgression requiring a slap on the wrist. And the powers that be had stacked the crowd in his favor. We do not know what happened to Barabbas after he was let go. We don't know if he felt that he, like Lazarus, had been raised from the dead and had a second chance at life. We don't know whether he changed his path in life, or whether he felt so beholden to those who had assured his release that he was unable to change his path.

After World War II, as psychologists began working with those who had survived the Holocaust, they discovered a phenomenon called the guilt of the survivor: the torment of being alive when all whom you had known and loved had died, the confusion over why you were still alive when so many others who were worthy had died. Did Barabbas feel this same sense of survivor guilt? That he had been freed at the expense of a life of another? Or was life so cheap to him that it didn't really matter? In a sense, Barabbas was the very first person that Jesus died to save. He was the most immediate beneficiary of Jesus' death.

WHEN WE SAY THAT JESUS DIED FOR US, that his death atoned for our sins, we tend to tip-toe around Jesus' death because we know the end of the story, we know that Jesus was raised from the dead and ascended to heaven. It somehow can seem to make the concept of Jesus' death a little softer, a little less real, a little less harsh and painful, and not really final. But Barabbas saw this death on his behalf first hand: he saw Jesus carrying the cross and he saw him die, if not in person, then in his mind, for crucifixions were a regular part of Roman occupied territory and Barabbas surely would have seen one for himself. Barabbas would clearly have known just what kind of death he had escaped.

A very important part of any commitment to Jesus involves a real understanding of what sin is, a sense of repentance for the sin in our life, and an under-standing of the atonement Jesus made for us. If we truly had that understanding, perhaps we would all be a good deal more humble, a good deal more gentle with each other, a good deal more committed.

*Lord, help us to see ourselves
in Barabbas's place —
as the one whose life was saved
because Jesus died for him.*

Soldiers Who Mocked Jesus

Matthew 27:27–31

Then the soldiers of the governor took Jesus into the praetorium, and they gathered the whole battalion before him. And they stripped him and put a scarlet robe upon him, and plaiting a crown of thorns they put it on his head, and put a reed in his right hand. And kneeling before him they mocked him, saying, "Hail King of the Jews!" And they spat upon him, and took the reed and struck him on the head. And when they had mocked him, they stripped him of the robe, and put his own clothes on him, and led him away to crucify him.

The soldiers, big, tough, burly men who were posted in this dusty desert city, charged with keeping an unruly, difficult population in line, sought entertainment where they could. The tenseness of the massive influx of crowds, more Jews from around the world, had all of them on edge. Armed revolts of the locals were never fun, and they were outnumbered. Perhaps even some new recruits had been brought into Jerusalem just for the Passover period, and new recruits were always dangerous, unaware of the local undercurrents, causing problems where none need be had. Still, a little horseplay never hurt.

So this condemned itinerant preacher was the King of the Jews? This was a play story even better than they could have come up with on their own! A king? Hah, they had seen what real kings were, and this bloodied character bore no relationship to the wealth, the cunning, the intrigue, the majesty of the emperors they had seen. Use some of that prickly bush over there in the corner to make a crown for this king. A cloak, a few pushes around the old courtyard, and then they would settle down to the business at hand, the crucifixion of this fellow. As for this "king's" religion, the belief system of these desert dwellers was of no concern or interest to them. What had it to do with the pomp, the beauty, the richness of the temples back in Rome, where the gods rode chariots across the sky and exuded beauty and power?

HOW LITTLE PEOPLE MATTER when they aren't people to us. When they are "other," "not like us," therefore "not human." Not real people who have wishes and dreams and hopes and families, with secrets and cherished memories — like ourselves. Prejudice and hatred have always required the dehumanization of the "other." Thus, whatever we do to this "not human" somehow doesn't count.

We now consider celebrities, figures in the news, and people who don't agree with us to be "not human," and therefore it really doesn't matter what private moments we peer into, what discussions we have about the intimate details of another's life, what glib, uninformed analyses we make of another person. They aren't real, they exist only for our entertainment, so we can do anything, say anything we want. In response, those so treated may learn to shut down, so that the slings and arrows that come their way don't hit so deeply. That part of them becomes not human, not real even to them.

The price we pay as individuals and as a society for this willingness to rob others of their humanity is very steep, for we learn to treat with callous contempt our fellow creations of God. This contempt, this willingness to so readily classify another as "not human" becomes an easy response, an easy way to dismiss rather than seek to know those who are different from us.

> *Help us, Lord, to watch*
> *what we say,*
> *what we think,*

how we act,
when we engage in denying other persons
the right to be equal children of yours.
Give us the commitment
to respect,
to explore,
and to accept differences,
to acknowledge that all people
are real in your eyes.

Crowds along the Path
to Golgotha

Luke 23:26–28

> *And as they led him away, they seized one Simon of Cyrene, who was coming in from the country, and laid on him the cross, to carry it behind Jesus. And there followed him a great multitude of the people, and of women who bewailed and lamented him. But Jesus turning to them said, "Daughters of Jerusalem, do not weep for me, but weep for yourselves and for your children...."*

We know that the Roman custom for a crucifixion was to take the condemned along as long a route as possible to the site of the execution so that as many as possible could see and learn in fear about the consequences of violating Roman law. It is probable that along the streets of Jerusalem crowds would cluster and watch in compassion or react in callousness to the criminal passing by. At this Passover time, when the city was strained to capacity and beyond, the streets must have been extremely crowded.

While all the Gospels describe the role of Simon of Cyrene, the bystander, in carrying the cross for Jesus, Luke is the only writer who tells the story of Jesus turning to address the women wailing for him as he went along the route to Golgotha. (Many commentators on this section describe the women as professional mourners.) If we picture any interaction at all between crowds and those who are condemned as criminals, we might think of catcalls or words of anger directed toward the prisoner, or of words of insult hurled back from the criminal to the crowd, but we never think of the criminal as pitying those in the crowd. Yet Jesus turns and tells the women not to wail for him, who is innocent, but for the city of Jerusalem; he then gives a prophetic warning of turmoil and disaster awaiting Jerusalem, which was in fact destroyed in 70 A.D. He speaks specifically of the sorrow of mothers during the disaster.

HOW WOULD WE REACT IF, when commiserating with another over a terrible occurrence, the victim turned to us and said, "I promise you, you and your family are next!" Would we not fall dumb with silence, taken aback, the tables suddenly turned as we immediately picture ourselves sitting in the other's place, stunned at what has happened, trying desperately to cope, now knowing exactly what it feels like? When Jesus paused on the sure route to death, he spoke not out of angry retaliation but out of pity, out of compassion. Think of the game of dominoes, when hundreds of dominoes are lined up, each ready to fall when the domino behind it falls forward. The chain reaction is slow and precise and inevitable. Just so, Jesus could say with certainty that the events had been set in motion, knowing that Jerusalem would be destroyed within decades of his death. Just as Jesus was facing his own terrible reality, his certain and soon death on the cross, so too did he know the wailing women would also one day face an inevitable future reality of their own, and the emotions they acted out that day would then be most terrifyingly real.

At times, we too are like that, going through the motions of expressing sorrow and joy and compassion, but inside too numb or too self-centered or too tired to really feel the emotions we express. But when our reality comes along, we feel, oh, how we feel. Now we know with great exactness how the other felt, now we wish our tears for them had been more genuine, more compassionate, as we realize how much we need and crave the shared emotion of others in our time of need.

Lord, let us acknowledge
the reality of each others' lives,
and commit to a ministry
of true compassion and sharing.

Jesus on the Way to Golgotha

Luke 23:26-28

And as they led him away, they seized one Simon of Cyrene, who was coming in from the country, and laid on him the cross, to carry it behind Jesus. And there followed him a great multitude of the people, and of women who bewailed and lamented him. But Jesus turning to them said, "Daughters of Jerusalem, do not weep for me, but weep for yourselves and for your children. . . . "

The scourging of a man by the Romans was a dreadful operation: the prisoner's back was exposed and a soldier flogged it with a leather thong studded with sharpened pieces of lead and bone. William Barclay says that the process literally tore a man's back to ribbons, that some died under it, and few retained consciousness through it.[9] According to John, Jesus was presented to the crowd by Pilate after being scourged, and then led away to be crucified, while the other Gospel writers have no such interval between the scourging and the forced march to Calvary. Jesus was called upon by the custom of execution in those days to carry his own cross. From the Praetorium to Golgotha, along narrow crowded streets, followed by curiosity seekers, Jewish authorities determined to see this through to the end, women followers of Jesus, and mere bystanders, Jesus struggled to carry the heavy wooden crossbar.

Jesus had grown up in the house of a carpenter, had become a carpenter himself, had known the ways of wood and how to coax useful and beautiful items from the harvest of the forest. But we can assume that never did Jesus use his skills to make an instrument of torture. The product of some other carpenter lay heavily, agonizingly on his back. Then, falling, unable to carry the bar any further, Jesus is given help from a Passover visitor, Simon of Cyrene.

THERE IS AN IMPLICIT and at times explicit assumption throughout the New Testament that part of being a follower of Jesus means carrying a cross, a unique cross that is allowed to be placed on our back by God, even if the cross is not of God's hands. It is not a question of "if" there will be times of darkness, times of difficulty and trials, but a question of "when." There is a tale that was told among the Jews in the concentration camps in World War II.

It was said that everyone in the world nailed on a tree all the sorrows of their own life. Then, when all of humanity had done so, each was allowed to go back to the tree and pick any sorrow they wanted, theirs or another's. And when it all was over, each person had chosen their own back again, for they knew them and could survive them. And so are we called to carry our own cross — but not alone, never alone.

Sometimes we build our own crosses. We engage in practices or habits that are at best unhealthy and at worst life-destroying. We treat those about us in a way that causes chaos, hurt, pain, and anger. We fail to use the gifts and opportunities we have been given. We see a way through but stubbornly stay put, preferring to nurse our grudges instead of moving on. Still other crosses are built for us and placed on our shoulders by life or genetics or circumstances not of our making. We are forced to trudge along, bowed under something that no one would ever say we deserved. And yet we are not alone. We are never alone. There is always God with us, who helps us carry the cross, to move forward, to find Simons who can carry the load with us.

> *God, help us bear the cross we have*
> *with a firm faith that at the end of our road*
> *lies life with you in glory.*

Simon of Cyrene

Mark 15:21–22

And they compelled a passerby, Simon of Cyrene, who was coming in from the country, the father of Alexander and Rufus, to carry his cross. And they brought him to the place called Golgotha (which means the place of a skull).

Romans 16:13

Greet Rufus, eminent in the Lord, also his mother and mine.

The day of the crucifixion seems like a long nightmare that will not end. From the Praetorium the soldiers took Jesus to be crucified. The Romans required that the criminal being crucified carry his own cross to the place of execution, surrounded by four soldiers, one of whom was carrying a board stating the criminal's crime. After being scourged, Jesus was hardly able to carry the weight of the cross. Perhaps he fell and, despite being whipped and beaten by the soldiers, could not stand and carry his cross. One of the Roman soldiers looked about, and as was his right, he touched Simon of Cyrene on the shoulder with the flat edge of his sword and pressed Simon into service.

A Jewish pilgrim from North Africa who had come to Jerusalem for the Passover, Simon may have been chosen because of his size or build or youth — a likely candidate who was capable of carrying a cross. Perhaps as he came out of the crowd, Simon looked at Jesus, and as their eyes met something in Jesus' eyes stirred something inside Simon. We wonder what Simon thought as he strained to carry the heavy cross along the long road, suddenly part of this unlikely series of events. If there were catcalls and shouting, perhaps Simon wanted to yell out that he wasn't the criminal, this wasn't his crucifixion. Almost certainly he would have wondered about the beaten and bloodied Christ walking ahead of him. Perhaps Simon stayed for the crucifixion, fascinated in spite of himself with the events so quickly unfolding, events in which he had now played a part. It is unlikely he received a handshake and hearty thanks from the soldiers for a job well done. Those with Simon, perhaps also not from Jerusalem, probably scrambled and pushed through the crowds, following the crucifixion route for fear of being separated from Simon. Thus, they too, out of concern and love for Simon, became part of the Passion story, suddenly drawn into this passing event as other plans were forced aside.

How do we come to know the name of this man, or who his sons were or where he was from? Since many biblical scholars connect Simon the Cyrene, the father of Rufus and Alexander, with the reference to Rufus, a stalwart of the faith, in Paul's letter to the Romans, perhaps this event for Simon became more than just a strange and unsettling event to be described to friends back home. Simon went to Jerusalem on a pilgrimage he may have waited his whole life to make, and then he carried a cross and his life was changed, and the lives of his family as well.

We too are asked to carry the cross of Jesus, and we too are told that when we carry the cross, our lives will also be transformed. Sometimes, like Simon, in the midst of following one dream, we find ourselves on a different path, one we didn't choose, and in that place we find our life's calling. What is the cross God calls us to carry, and where will that journey as a cross-carrier take us?

God, give us the strength and the courage
to carry the cross we are given
and the wisdom to use the experience
to transform our lives
and the lives of those around us.

The Merciful Women
of Jerusalem

Matthew 27:33-34

*And when they came to a place called Golgotha
(which means the place of a skull), they offered
him wine to drink, mingled with gall; but when
he tasted it, he would not drink it.*

When Jesus arrived at the place where he was to be
crucified he was offered wine mixed with frankincense, which was intended to deaden the pain of the
crucified one. We are told by Jewish writings of the
time that a group of wealthy, pious Jewish women
in Jerusalem bought the ingredients for and prepared
this drink as an act of mercy.

We can imagine this small but dedicated group
of women. Perhaps a relative or a friend's relative's
son was crucified and one of the women saw with
pity and horror the pain of a death by crucifixion.
Perhaps this one pondered what could be done —

perhaps the herbs used to ease the pain of child-birth or at other times could be provided. But, would the Romans allow it? How did they secure approval from the authorities? Perhaps one day they just began to provide this act of compassion and the soldiers lacked the will to stop them. The Gospel writers do not tell us who offered the wine to the condemned, for many in this part of the story lack a name or description. But we can imagine the wine being offered to a man whose hands will imminently be nailed to the cross, who is just beginning to comprehend the pain he will be forced to endure; perhaps a word, a tender touch, and the cup being held to the lips. Even now, even now, you are not alone, the unspoken message was given.

Henri Nouwen and his coauthors write in their book *Compassion* that the word "compassion" comes from the Latin, meaning "to suffer with." They write:

> Compassion asks us to go where it hurts, to enter into places of pain, to share in broken-ness, fear, confusion, and anguish. Compassion challenges us to cry out with those in misery, to mourn with those who are lonely, to weep with those in tears....Compassion means full immersion in the condition of being human.[10]

These women, who had no name, who merited no mention, nonetheless administered compassion to the least of all. There was no possibility of ever being "paid back" in kind, or having a favor returned. They would not see the objects of their ministrations get better or turn their lives around. It was compassion in action in the purest sense to those who had no advocates.

WE SO OFTEN WANT SOMETHING in response to our acts of charity. We want our limited time and resources to go to those who are worthy, or those whose innocent lives have been destroyed by others or by illness. We seldom seek out the guilty, the unrepentant, the condemned, the unconverted, and minister to them with no thought of "success." Have we become so conscious of the bottom line, of the need to show results, that we overlook those unlikely to provide a "return on our investment" and fail to realize that even these need compassion?

Help us, God,
to seek out those who are most alone
and most in need,
help us to learn to give
even where there is no chance of any return.
Help us to see your child in every human being.

Jesus' Followers at the Foot of the Cross

Mark 15:40–41

There were also women looking on from afar, among whom were Mary Magdalene, and Mary the mother of James the younger and of Joses, and Salome, who, when he was in Galilee, followed him, and ministered to him; and also many other women who came up with him to Jerusalem.

Outside the confines of the city, the hill is steep and rocky, the occasional bits of earth flattened by the pounding of feet, and the grass growing in small, stubbornly tenacious clumps, sunbaked to a tepid brown. The soldiers mill about, rudely joking to relieve the oppressiveness of this duty, to keep the demon at bay. Jesus' followers, mostly the women, sit in groups, defeated, stunned, resigned, weeping, helpless. The inability to change anything, the sense of being swept along in some inexorable movement that leads toward death is heavy in the air. In spite of the heat, the stillness of air that won't move, the women feel cold, the fingers tremble for wanting to soothe the brow of the man they loved, for wanting to bring it all to some merciful end, for wanting to cling to his life, but also wanting the breath of life to disappear quickly so the agony would be over.

As horrifying as this was, this was still a world with Jesus in it, and no one who loved Jesus wanted to face what the world would be like the minute after Jesus died, when the world suddenly did not have Jesus in it. For everything would change, and they knew it. The presence of God would no longer be just at hand in the same way. No longer could they take the very problems of their life and hear the voice of God's son telling them how to think about a concern, or what new way of bringing God into the everyday could happen. How would it be when they could no longer hear Jesus' voice, see his intense gaze, know that, somehow, this rabbi was the one person in all of life they could count on to do what was right, be what was right, be the voice, the action, the thought of God working out in front of them? There probably was no thought at this point that God through Jesus was also living out their own lives in front of them. That God was forever going to know what it was like to feel hunger, thirst, to know the warmth of friendship and the pain of betrayal, to know the agony of mockery and torturous death. That never again could humans doubt that God knows exactly what their lives are like. That God had brought eternity and humanity into coexistent understanding.

IN THE BACKGROUND OF JESUS' PUBLIC MINISTRY are many women who provided for Jesus and his disciples. The failure to record their conversations with Jesus or even their names does not mean the relationships were inconsequential or trivial. And it was they, not the disciples, who were present at the end, when there was only a sense of ultimate sorrow and loss, a sense of darkness that overshadowed the whole world. In the depths of our own times of separation from God, all we know is Good Friday, all we see is the body taken down from the cross, the absence of Jesus' living and breathing presence in our world. We do not see Easter Sunday, we do not know resurrection, we do not know the joy of knowing a God who knows us. We only know a stone rolled in front of a tomb that will never be rolled away.

> *Lord, help us to enter into this darkness,*
> *to know fully this absence of Jesus,*
> *for then and only then can we truly know*
> *the joy of Easter morning.*

The Soldiers Who Gambled

John 19:23–25a

*When the soldiers had crucified Jesus they took
his garments and made four parts, one for each
soldier; also his tunic. But the tunic was without
seam, woven from top to bottom; so they said to
one another, "Let us not tear it, but cast lots for
it to see whose it shall be." This was to fulfill
the scripture,*

> *"They parted my garments among them,
> and for my clothing they cast lots."*

So the soldiers did this.

A criminal on the way to a crucifixion was guarded
by four soldiers. One of the perks of these soldiers,
who remained at the site of the execution, was the
clothes of the condemned. For a Jew, there were
five pieces of clothing: shoes, turban, girdle, tunic,
and outer robe. As the soldiers played a game of
chance, the winner picked an article of clothing. Left

at the end was Jesus' tunic, a seamless tunic of the kind priests wore. We recoil from the picture created by John's account: soldiers gambling for Jesus' clothing at the foot of the cross on which Jesus was dying. Perhaps it is the callousness, the indifference, the boredom in the presence of death that so strikes us, or perhaps it is the sense that the indignities heaped on Jesus never seemed to have stopped even at the end. Jesus died with only his loincloth to call his own.

I NDIFFERENCE. Throughout the Passion story, we see a wide range of emotions expressed in connection with Jesus: the love and devotion of the women who followed Jesus, the betrayal of Judas, the fierce and all-consuming hatred of the chief priests and scribes, jubilant crowds, a perplexed and cornered Roman ruler, mocking soldiers, fearful and passionate disciples, a grieving mother. But we have not seen indifference, the kind of indifference that extended beyond a particular person or a specific event to almost a callousness, an inability to feel a spark of human empathy. It is hard to get the attention of one filled with this kind of indifference, of those absorbed solely with making sure they get what is owed to them, even if it is only a dusty pair of sandals or a sweat-stained, blood-spattered, road-weary tunic. There is a hardness of heart that falls short of the blaze of hatred; this is a hardness that refuses to pay attention, that has grown weary of hard times, sad stories, lost futures, and crippled lives. If I don't pay attention, I don't have to feel, I don't have to act, I don't have to rattle the confines of the safe world I have built for myself. When we are on the Cross Road, though, we are called to see, to look at the crosses borne by fellow humans, to feel the call for help, and to reach out from the Christ in us to the Christ in them. Fellow wounded travelers on the Cross Road all, we minister to the suffering Jesus by caring for the suffering in our world.

Lord, keep our hearts soft, open to your appeal
to love the wounded and the cross-bearers.
Help us to keep from nailing you
to the cross again by our indifference
to those whom you died to save.

The Thief on the Cross
Who Believed

Luke 23:32–33, 39–43

Two others also, who were criminals, were led away to be put to death with him. And when they came to the place which is called The Skull, there they crucified him, and the criminals, one on the right and one on the left....

One of the criminals who were hanged railed at him, saying, "Are you not the Christ? Save yourself and us!" But the other rebuked him, saying, "Do you not fear God, since you are under the same sentence of condemnation? And we indeed justly; for we are receiving the due reward of our deeds; but this man has done nothing wrong." And he said, "Jesus, remember me when you come in your kingdom." And he said to him, "Truly, I say to you, today you will be with me in Paradise."

At the end of his life, Jesus was crucified between two robbers, one at his right and one at his left. We cannot help but think of the petitions from James and John and the arguing among the disciples over who was to be at the right and the left hand of Jesus when he entered his kingdom. The answer, of course, is that even at his death, Jesus found his place with the sinners. Matthew, Mark, and John all join Luke in telling us that both robbers joined the religious authorities in reviling Jesus, even as he was dying on the cross. Luke alone gives us this portrait of the thief who came to believe in Jesus.

We know nothing about this man other than his crime; there is no mention of a family watching in horrified silence or bewildered grieving as his death sentence was carried out. We do not read that the Romans called upon others along the route up to Golgotha to help either of the two thieves with their heavy burden. Perhaps the thieves had been in prison for a while, awaiting their sentence. Perhaps they learned who Jesus was from prison guards, or were moved by the crowd of followers that accompanied Jesus to Golgotha. Perhaps they were struck by the manner in which he accepted what was happening to him. For whatever reason, then, this thief now was prepared to believe in Jesus. His very request is humble: "When you come into your kingdom remember me." In the midst of his own agony, his own end-of-life thoughts and prayers to whatever gods he may have believed in, he turned to Jesus. Perhaps he was one who never in his everyday life of petty and great crime would have spared a thought to matters of the hereafter, matters of faith and questions of religion. Perhaps he was one for whom the moment was everything, whatever was happening now was what counted. But on that day, at that time, he saw the future and he saw Jesus, he knew that the soul was real and that the hereafter mattered, and he knew that Jesus was paradise-bound.

A T WHAT POINT DO WE TAKE GOD SERIOUSLY? At what point does our soul, our eternal life begin to get our attention? What has to happen to us, how far does our life have to go astray, what is required to shake us out of our complacency to get us to pay attention to God? We so often tread water, equidistant between two shores, with little concern over where we are going, convinced that at some unknown point in the future we will have time to sit down and "figure it all out." And yet, when we get to our most extreme point, will we be able to recognize the face of God? Would we, crucified on a cross that is the result of our own actions, be able to look at the fellow on the cross next to us and recognize our Savior? Or have we been so long in the faith, so placid in our thinking, that over time, the face we imagine of God has come to resemble our own?

God, help us to see
that when our actions have taken us to a cross,
or even when our successes have taken us
to the lonely top of the mountain,
you are there, waiting for us,
meeting us in the guise of a fellow sinner
so that we may dare to approach you
and ask for mercy.

The Second Thief
on the Cross

Luke 23:32–33, 39–43

Two others also, who were criminals, were led away to be put to death with him. And when they came to the place which is called The Skull, there they crucified him, and the criminals, one on the right and one on the left. . . .

One of the criminals who were hanged railed at him, saying, "Are you not the Christ? Save yourself and us!" But the other rebuked him, saying, "Do you not fear God, since you are under the same sentence of condemnation? And we indeed justly; for we are receiving the due reward of our deeds; but this man has done nothing wrong." And he said, "Jesus, remember me when you come in your kingdom." And he said to him, "Truly, I say to you, today you will be with me in Paradise."

After traveling together down that long road to Golgotha, after watching their clothes be divided up among their executioners, Jesus and two robbers were crucified. All three were offered wine with some frankincense in it, intended to deaden the excruciating pain of death on the cross, which had been known to take up to a week before the condemned finally died of hunger and thirst. Unhappily, crucifixions would not have been a rare occurrence, and the two robbers would have been aware of the kind of death that awaited them. Only in Luke do we have an extended account of the interaction of the robbers between themselves and with Jesus.

The reactions of people to terrible situations are seldom predictable: some react with anger and rage, needing to lash out, find someone to blame for whatever is happening; others crumple entirely and fade into useless whimpering and wailing, while others find internal reservoirs of resolve and strength, dignity and courage. The second thief clearly fell into the first category, managing even then to be a bully, a tyrant, finding a way to put down a fellow condemned man to prove that even at the bottom of the heap, he could find or make someone be still lower. His shell had grown so tough, the self-reliance was so thorough, the distrust and the cynicism and the deep knowledge of the rotten places in life were too strong to allow him even then to see uncorrupted innocence.

Joining with the chief priests and scribes, the thief mocked and reviled Jesus. Then he probably cursed God and begged for death.

W E CREATE OUR OWN DARK PLACES. We paint our windows black and block out the light. We lock our doors, bar our entrances and exits, refuse to let anyone in, and become captives to our own fear. We see in others whatever proves our own view of the world; we find in the world that which we condemn. Alternative ways of seeing need not apply. Yet, it is a choice, how we choose to see the world and what we find in it. Even when the worst of life and of other people happen to us, even when we are crushed beneath the weight of our own lives, we can still keep the windows open, we can still choose to find a tiny place for the light to live and begin to grow and cleanse and bathe all the hurts and gangrenous places in our lives with healing power.

It is often said that while we cannot always choose what will happen to us, we can choose to control how we will react to what happens to us. One way, the second thief's way, of reacting is to spit back in the eye of the one who is responsible for what has happened to us. To give back what you got. And, if it helps to blame God for the evil that has befallen you, what greater sense of power than to snarl and curse the hand of the Almighty. Yet, blaming God for all that has happened can be a way of evading personal and collective responsibility for the choices that have been made.

Help us, God,
to choose light even when surrounded by darkness,
to choose you even when life overwhelms us,
and to choose Life when we face death.

John, the Beloved Disciple

John 13:21–28

When Jesus had thus spoken, he was troubled in spirit, and testified, "Truly, truly, I say to you, one of you will betray me." The disciples looked at one another, uncertain of whom he spoke. One of his disciples, whom Jesus loved, was lying close to the breast of Jesus; so Simon Peter beckoned to him and said, "Tell us who it is of whom he speaks." So lying thus, close to the breast of Jesus, he said to him, "Lord who is it?" Jesus answered, "It is he to whom I shall give this morsel when I have dipped it." So, when he had dipped the morsel, he gave it to Judas, the son of Simon Iscariot. Then after the morsel, Satan entered into him. Jesus said to him, "What you are going to do, do quickly." Now no one at the table knew why he had said this to him.

John 19:25b–27

But standing by the cross of Jesus were his mother, and his mother's sister, Mary the wife of Clopas, and Mary Magdalene. When Jesus saw his mother, and the disciple whom he loved standing near, he said to his mother, "Woman, behold your son!" Then he said to the disciple, "Behold, your mother!" And from that hour the disciple took her to his own home.

John, who is believed by some to be Jesus' cousin, is often described in the Gospels as the disciple whom Jesus loved. John is present at several key points throughout the Passion story: the Last Supper, in the Garden, at the foot of the cross. Because we know that Jesus loved him, we have higher expectations for John, we believe he should have better understood what Jesus was saying, been braver in his defense of Jesus, been unhampered by fear or hesitation. We place on John all our expectations of what the disciples should have been, should have done, should have understood throughout the last weeks of Jesus' life. John was the one to whom Jesus confided at the Last Supper that "the one who dips his bread with me at the same time shall betray me," and we wonder why John did not act, why he did not stand up and rush to stop Judas or immediately share what

Jesus told him with the rest of the disciples. We then see John in the Garden of Gethsemane with the other disciples, but we read that he too fell asleep.

At the same time we feel disappointment at John's failure to act as we would want him to, we also feel comforted by the presence of John. We know that Jesus was not entirely alone, that he had a friend in whom he could confide the best hopes and the worst fears, the small things that Jesus knew would happen but was reluctant to tell all the disciples. Jesus had a friend who mattered to him. And so we see John, alone of all the disciples, at the foot of the cross. Jesus asks John to take care of his mother Mary, to care for her as if she were John's own mother, establishing the new family of believers where faith and relationship to Jesus create new connections, new relationships, new communities.

C AN WE EVER SEE THE REALITY of the one we love the most? Does the loved one become invincible in our eyes, because we can't imagine life without the beloved alive? Did John think that Jesus was telling him about distant future events, but not necessarily an event that would happen within hours? How often do we really want to hear what our friends have to tell us? A friend tries to tell us of her fear of dying as she has just received word that she has breast cancer; we immediately are dismissive of her fears — "You'll be fine. You're not going to die," we say. After a man loses his job and says he has no idea what will happen to his family, we are quick to say, "Oh, you'll find a job. Don't worry."

Why do we push away another's concern? If we allow a friend to voice fear, then it means we have to face that fear ourselves as well, and we aren't ready to do that. We seek to avoid pain at all costs for we believe that pain has nothing to teach us that we want to learn. We fear the presence of loss in our lives, so we pretend, and we are irritated if the friend won't help maintain this facade. But when the fear becomes unavoidable reality, the willingness to play such games falls away, and all we want is to be able to speak honestly, and a friend who will listen and bear that honesty, honor the pain and the fear we feel by not diminishing it or pretending it will go away.

> *God, help us to be a friend*
> *who can hear reality,*
> *even when it scares us.*

Mary, Mother of Jesus

John 19:25b

But standing by the cross of Jesus were his mother, and his mother's sister, Mary the wife of Clopas, and Mary Magdalene.

John is the only Gospel that places Mary, mother of Jesus, at the crucifixion. We are transfixed by the spiritual journey that Mary has made in her life. The Gospels relate several appearances of Mary during Jesus' adult ministry. We think of the wedding at Cana where Mary had a calm expectation that her son would know about and would be able to resolve the problem of the wine running out, or we remember the time when Mary and Jesus' brothers came to see him and Jesus turned them away, asking, "Who is my mother and who are my brothers?" There may have been some confusion on Mary's part, watching Jesus assume the role he had been born for, teaching and leading and confronting, surrounded always by crowds and followers. Perhaps Mary feared for her firstborn. Perhaps she longed to see him more, or felt cheated by all the others who now stood between her and her son.

The separation of parents and adult children can be a hard adjustment. But then, at the end, there is Mary at the foot of the cross, powerless to protect her child from harm. The unimaginable, unendurable pain of seeing her child put to death in front of her for unknown crimes, for incomprehensible reasons, for a purpose she could not fathom. The deep, searing love of a mother for her child, the intangible but steel-strong bond that extends from the bearer of life to the life created. Did a stunned and numb Mary desperately wish that somehow, this whole nightmare would end and she would wake and find Jesus once again hanging on to her knee, looking up at her with the absolute trust of a young child?

What do we do when we can no longer bear that which we must bear? Did Mary's faith ever waver when Jesus was on the cross? Did she relive the annunciation from the angel Gabriel and wonder if perhaps she had misunderstood, somehow tragically gotten it all wrong? Did she doubt in this her darkest hour the faith that had carried her so long?

THE MARY AT THE FOOT OF THE CROSS is different from the Mary in the stable in Bethlehem. The Mary at the manger is suffused with hope, with all the fervor of a young mother awed and mystified by the power of new life. The Mary at the foot of the cross knows the pain that love opens us up to, the shattering, crumpling pain that can happen when we give part of ourselves into the keeping of another. Yet the Mary at the foot of the cross is also the face of dignity that has been earned when suffering has been endured. Those who follow Jesus and have counted the cost of faith, those who have dared to love without limits and have trusted God to heal the wounds of love lost can have a depth, a strength, an innate tenderness toward others that those who have followed the star to the babe in the manger but have never been on the Cross Road do not show. When love has been tested, when faith has been tried by the deep waters, when a heart has been broken after love has opened it to others, our lives and our faith reflect our time as cross-carriers.

God, let us find the strength
to see through this present test,
this present suffering,
to the trust we first placed in you,
the faith we know you are worthy of.
Help us to know that you will never leave us.

The Centurion

Matthew 27:51–54

And behold, the curtain of the temple was torn in two, from top to bottom; and the earth shook, and the rocks were split; the tombs also were opened, and many bodies of the saints who had fallen asleep were raised, and coming out of the tombs after his resurrection they went into the holy city and appeared to many. When the centurion and those who were with him, keeping watch over Jesus, saw the earthquake and what took place, they were filled with awe, and said, "Truly this was the Son of God!"

A Roman centurion commanded one hundred soldiers. While he did not have all one hundred soldiers with him on this day, his presence at the crucifixion was a sign of its importance to the Roman government. The assignment to crucifixion duty, especially during the unstable period of Passover, was merely one more bad job in a difficult posting. The centurion would have picked up Jesus and the other two criminals from the Praetorium and overseen their march to Golgotha. The shouting, jostling crowd, the wailing women, and the rough breathing of the prisoners as they carried their crossbars would have created a tension in the soldiers. Perhaps the centurion had overseen many crucifixions, for it was unlikely that this sentence at this time would have been carried out by one new to the process.

Still, he had never seen a prisoner where the charge was "King of the Jews," or where the prisoner drew such cries and taunts from chief priests. He had never seen a prisoner refuse the pain-deadening drink of mercy offered to those sentenced to die on the cross. And he had never had a criminal at the time of crucifixion say, "Father, forgive them for they know not what they do," a statement that had added to the surreal quality of this matter. There was much that compelled this hard-bitten, battle-toughened leader to ponder the prisoner Jesus. Even the earth seemed to grieve for this man. An unexplainable darkness had settled over the land about noon, causing the superstitious soldiers to look uneasily about themselves, unsure what was happening, becoming acutely attentive where boredom had been. Then, when Jesus died, even the very stones of the earth were convulsed by an earthquake. The centurion as well felt shaken to the depths of his soul.

T HE SPONTANEOUS STATEMENT of the centurion, "Truly this was the Son of God," is meant to reflect what reaction the cross should bring. It is as if the recognition of Jesus' death alone, that miracle of the absolute sacrificial offering, even without the resurrection to come, should compel us to believe that Jesus was who he said he was.

Sometimes, we are unable to see the power in what is happening about us until it is over. We get caught up in accomplishing tasks, checking off lists, attending meetings, taking care of our part of the whole. Then, when it all comes to fruition, we stand back and see it all, see what was dreamed of, planned for, sacrificed for, come to life and we are awed in spite of ourselves. We are meant to see the cross and recognize Jesus; we are meant to see the whole of his life, his ministry, his message, his living model of God to us suddenly come down to one idea: this was the Son of God and this is what he did for us. Who can really see such a miracle and turn away unmoved?

God help us, like the centurion,
to see Jesus' life and death as a whole,
as a miracle for us,
intended to turn our hearts,
our whole beings to you.
Let us seek to understand, and understanding,
let us voice belief in your amazing love for us.

Joseph of Arimathea

Luke 23:50–54

Now there was a man named Joseph from the Jewish town of Arimathea. He was a member of the council, a good and righteous man, who had not consented to their purpose and deed, and he was looking for the kingdom of God. This man went to Pilate and asked for the body of Jesus. Then he took it down and wrapped it in a linen shroud, and laid him in a rock-hewn tomb, where no one had ever yet been laid. It was the day of Preparation and the sabbath was beginning.

We actually don't come upon Joseph of Arimathea until after the cross, when he went to Pontius Pilate and asked for Jesus' body so that it could be buried in a tomb that Joseph had set aside. Despite his late appearance in the story, however, we know that Joseph must have been a player in the Passion story, for we are told that he was a member of the Sanhedrin and that he had not voted with the rest of the members for Jesus' death. However, we also have no record of him raising his voice in dissent at the meeting of the Sanhedrin or at any point throughout the numerous proceedings. Perhaps he could not believe that what the Sanhedrin did would actually lead to the events that unfolded. If such was the case, he must have spent a great deal of time thinking about "If only..." in the hours that followed Jesus' condemnation to death.

Joseph is often characterized as a wealthy, powerful follower of Jesus who lacked the courage to stand up for or to acknowledge the fact he followed the rabbi Jesus. We see that Joseph had some political clout because he was actually able to see Pontius Pilate and have his request granted. One of the most common maxims of political life is to be careful how you spend your political "capital" — you can ask for favors, concessions, or attention only so many times before you run out of your political "chips." Then you owe everyone and can ask for nothing in return. Yet some lose power because they never spend the political capital they have. And so the question arises, what if he had tried to use his political chips before Jesus' death? There is a sense about the figure of Joseph that he helped out too late. He failed to grasp the significance of the events that were swirling about him, as if he tried to pretend that it would all somehow just go away — only it didn't.

W E OFTEN SHRUG OUR SHOULDERS when faced with the seemingly endless litany of ills that need correction in the world. "Oh, what can one person do anyway?" we say. At the same time, we see so many examples of what one person can do for evil in the world — the havoc a Hitler or a Stalin can wreak on an era. And we think of Mother Teresa, who inspired a world to care about the poorest of the poor.

We have power when we think we have power. We have the power at every moment of our lives to act for good or for evil. We have the ability to step forward, to make the world a kinder, gentler place, to replace the snarled comment with the supportive statement. We do have the power to light a single candle in the darkness if we choose to. It is not that Joseph of Arimathea lacked power; it is that he failed to use what he did have.

God, help us to begin to step out in your name,
to become your hands,
to lend to your work what we have,
no matter how small or insignificant
we may think our effort is.

Help us to understand
that taking that step is what begins to teach us
that we can take the next step and the next.
As we change ourselves,
so we become the person
who can make a difference
for good in the world today.

Easter Saturday

Luke 23:56b

On the sabbath they rested according to the commandment.

After the body of Jesus had been taken down from the cross and handed over to Joseph of Arimathea and a very brief burial preparation had been undertaken, Jesus' body was placed in the tomb and his followers hurried home to observe the Sabbath. That Jewish Sabbath was what we now would call Holy Saturday or Easter Saturday. On that day, the disciples were hiding in the upper room, fearful of the Jews, distraught and afraid, lost and purposeless, out of sorts with each other and life, filled with immense questions about their own future as well as the "cause" to which they had devoted their past several years. Some may have sat in corners of the room, staring into space, pondering without allowing their minds to settle on any thought for very long. Others may have argued among themselves over what happened or what they should have done or what Jesus should have done differently. Everyone handles grief and tension and anger in different ways.

Then, on the first day of the week, the women hurried down to the tomb and found the stone rolled away.

HOLY SATURDAY HAS A UNIQUE CHARACTER of its own, not quite into the rejoicing of Easter, not quite out of the sorrow of Good Friday. As we ponder this, we realize how very wonderful it was that the resurrection came after three short days. What if the resurrection had not happened for three weeks; or three months or three years? How would the disciples have felt and acted if the span of time were much greater than three days? How long would it have been before they eventually left their hiding place? Would they have stayed friends afterward? Would they have pretended they had never followed Jesus? What occupation would they have returned to? Would their faith have faded and grown into but a dim memory over time? In *The Lion, the Witch, and the Wardrobe,* the first book of C. S. Lewis's Narnia series for children, Lewis describes Narnia as a place where it was "always winter and never Christmas."[11] What if it were always Holy Saturday and never Easter?

Our own resurrection experiences seldom come three days after our Good Friday experiences. Our resurrections seem to take a longer time. We recover slowly from loss, we reclaim our sense of self-confidence in bits and pieces, and it takes awhile, sometimes a long while, for the spring in our step, our ability to be more open and direct, our ability to believe again, to recover. And during that time, when the processes of healing and coming back to life are working so slowly, so tentatively, and often so secretly, we may despair of the reality of a resurrection experience.

God, help us to grow out of our Good Fridays
and into our Easter Sundays,
whether it takes us three days or three years.
Guide us as we choose whether to hide
in fear and hopelessness as the disciples did,
with no knowledge
that in the midst of their despair
you were working to roll back the stone,
or to look forward with confidence and faith
that there is the bright dawning light
of the resurrection ahead
for each of us.

Notes

1. Lloyd J. Ogilvie, *Life without Limits: The Message of Mark's Gospel* (Waco, TX: Word Books, 1975), 212, 214.

2. Ibid., 213.

3. William Barclay, *The Gospel of Luke,* rev. ed. (Philadelphia: The Westminster Press, 1975), 235.

4. William Barclay, *The Gospel of Matthew,* rev. ed. (Philadelphia: The Westminster Press, 1975), 2:230–31.

5. Mary Stewart-Wilson, *Queen Mary's Dolls' House* (London: Ebury Press, 1988), 10.

6. William Barclay, *The Gospel of John* (Edinburgh: The Saint Andrew Press, 1955), 1:204.

7. Carol A. Newsom and Sharon H. Ringe, eds., *The Women's Bible Commentary* (Louisville: Westminster/John Knox Press, 1992), 273.

8. Barclay, *The Gospel of John,* 2:263–66.

9. William Barclay, *The Gospel of Mark,* rev. ed. (Philadelphia: The Westminster Press, 1975), 358.

10. Donald P. McNeill, Douglas A. Morrison, and Henri J. M. Nouwen, *Compassion: A Reflection on the Christian Life* (New York: Doubleday, 1982), 4.

11. C. S. Lewis, *The Lion, the Witch, and the Wardrobe* (New York: Macmillan, 1950), 47.